THE PRISON OF WOMANHOOD

The Prison of Womanhood

Four Provincial Heroines in Nineteenth-Century Fiction

Elizabeth Jean Sabiston
Academic Advisor, Stong College
York University, Toronto

St. Martin's Press
New York

© Elizabeth Jean Sabiston 1987

All rights reserved. For information write:
Scholarly & Reference Division,
St. Martin's Press, Inc., 175 Fifth Avenue, New York, NY 10010

First published in the United States of America in 1987

Printed in Hong Kong

ISBN 0-312-00081-2

Library of Congress Cataloging-in-Publication Data
Sabiston, Elizabeth Jean, 1937–
The prison of womanhood.
Includes index.
1. English fiction – 19th century – History and criticism.   2. Women in
literature.   3. Heroines in literature.   4. Imprisonment in literature.   5.
English fiction – Women authors – History and criticism.   6. Women and
literature – Great Britain.   7. Flaubert, Gustave, 1821–1880. Madame
Bovary.   8. James, Henry, 1843–1916. Portrait of a lady.   I. Title.
PR868.W6S23   1987   823'.7'09352042   86–20281
ISBN 0-312-00081-2

For my dear father
who encouraged me to achieve like a son
but loved me more than a son

For my darling mother
the strongest woman I know

For Hédi
who has been with me every step of the way

Contents

Acknowledgements

A previous version of Chapter 1 was published as 'The Prison of Womanhood' in *Comparative Literature*, xxv, 4 (Fall 1973) 336–51. I should like to acknowledge the help of my students, undergraduate and graduate, who helped shape my thinking while I worked on this book, with special thanks to Terri Doughty, Marlene Richman and Phyllis Rozendal for invaluable assistance in preparing the final copy.

1

'Emma's Daughters': a Study in Isolation and Creativity

Henry James's description of 'a certain young woman affronting her destiny' first appeared in 1881:

> Altogether, with her meagre knowledge, her inflated ideals, her confidence at once innocent and dogmatic, her temper at once exacting and indulgent, her mixture of curiosity and indifference, her desire to look very well and to be if possible even better, her determination to see, to try, to know, her combination of the delicate, desultory, flame-like spirit and the eager and personal creature of conditions, she would be an easy victim of scientific criticism if she were not intended to awaken on the reader's part an impulse more tender and more purely expectant.[1]

To contemporary society, increasingly concerned with the 'emancipated' woman and her functions outside the 'doll's house' – a concern manifested in works ranging from Sinclair Lewis's *Main Street* to Betty Friedan's *The Feminine Mystique*, Kate Millett's *Sexual Politics*, Germaine Greer's *The Female Eunuch* and Elizabeth Janeway's *Man's World, Woman's Place* – James's Isabel Archer seems to be the prototype of recent portraits of young women who are vaguely ambitious, dissatisfied, yearning to escape from some intangible prison to – they know not what.

If James does not actually originate the conception, he has nevertheless, with his usual acuteness, defined for us in one sentence the whole problem of a certain type of heroine. She is the victim not only of the conflict between herself and the external world, but also of a tension between opposites in her own character: an idealism uninformed by knowledge of reality, and particularly of evil; a thirst for experience coupled with fastidiousness and a

1

tendency to surrender to outside forces. The author immediately informs us of his own point of view by cautioning the reader to care for her, not to judge her scientifically. It is clear even in this passage that James himself combines ironic detachment, if not 'scientific criticism', with great tenderness for Isabel. His mingled irony and tenderness are easily traceable not only to his inevitable sympathy with her creative, imaginative instincts, but also to his realistic assessment of the frustrations imposed on her by her narrow background and by her own blindness to certain aspects of human existence.

James's brief summary of Isabel's character, of her prospects for fulfilment, and of the likelihood of her ultimate frustration almost immediately follows his presentation of his heroine alone in the 'office' of her grandmother's house in Albany. The scene in Albany suggests the source of Isabel's 'inflated ideals' and of 'her confidence at once innocent and dogmatic', as well as the reasons underlying the meagreness of her knowledge. Her isolation as a young girl has been both geographical and spiritual, both imposed on her from without and a matter of her own choosing. It has failed to provide her imagination with concrete materials on which to work, but at the same time it has provided ample space for her imagination to soar unchecked.

Even prior to Mrs Touchett's discovery of her niece in 'the office', Isabel has, in fact, lived in cosmopolitan New York and travelled in Europe with her father. But her spiritual and moral home is the old house in Albany, which resembles 'a bustling provincial inn kept by a gentle old landlady' (*Portrait*, p. 32), and particularly the 'mysterious melancholy' of 'the office', whose restrictions set free her imagination when she was a child, and have retained their appeal for the adult:

> The place owed much of its mysterious melancholy to the fact that it was properly entered from the second door of the house, the door that had been condemned. ... She knew that this silent, motionless portal opened into the street; if the sidelights had not been filled with green paper she might have looked out upon the little brown stoop and the well-worn brick pavement. But she had no wish to look out, for this would have interfered with her theory that there was a strange, unseen place on the other side – a place which became to the child's imagination, according to its different moods, a region of delight or of terror.   (*Portrait*, p. 33)

Later, throughout the entire series of European houses in which Isabel's explorations of life take place – Gardencourt, Lockleigh, the Roccanera – the reader always retains his initial impression that Isabel's spiritual affinities are with provincial Albany, whose moral standards and innocence she invincibly maintains in the face of an older and often corrupt culture.

For many readers the mental image of Isabel Archer shut off from the world in the house in Albany, engrossed in her reading of George Eliot and Robert Browning, epitomises the imaginative provincial woman. Isabel is not, however, as Henry James himself was well aware, the first imaginative provincial heroine in prose fiction. Her predecessors include, perhaps most notably, Jane Austen's Emma Woodhouse, Gustave Flaubert's Emma Bovary and George Eliot's Dorothea Brooke. Emma Woodhouse is in many ways the prototype of the creative provincial, self-deceived and mentally blind who, in trying to rise above her society, often merely reinforces its values. Emma Bovary and Dorothea Brooke are the central figures in novels whose subtitles proclaim them to be respectively a picture of the *Moeurs de province* and *A Study of Provincial Life*.

All four novelists focus upon a woman trying against insurmountable odds, like a Conradian hero, to realise her 'ideal conception of her own personality'. The basic components in all four of these variations on the provincial theme would seem to be a society which imposes even more severe limitations upon women than upon men; and, as the protagonist, an imaginative heroine, nourished upon books rather than upon life, and given to flights of fancy. In all cases the heroine's 'provincialism' has both positive and negative aspects, for it prompts her to seek ultimate values, but at the same time imposes an ignorance upon her which prevents her from ever attaining them. Because her isolation and ignorance are only in part a matter of her own choice, she is, in the words of the Sartrean epigraph to Simone de Beauvoir's *Le Deuxième Sexe*, 'A moitié victime, à moitié complice, comme tout le monde.' Finally, the tension in her between aspiration and ignorance dictates her author's mixture of tenderness and irony towards her; even, at times, predisposes him to judge her actions by the same criteria he might apply to his own artistic endeavours.

A tradition of romantic, imaginative, provincial heroines exists within the 'great tradition' of prose fiction. Its nature can best be revealed through a close reading of *Emma, Madame Bovary,*

Middlemarch and *The Portrait of a Lady*.[2] Although there are many other representatives of the tradition, these four have been selected because they are, in an important sense, the most 'successful' because their authors most fully render and develop the theme of the imaginative provincial woman.

Although several critics have mentioned that the four heroines – the two Emmas, Dorothea and Isabel – and a few others related to the tradition are almost fictional sisters, they have neither explored the question in depth, nor systematised their conclusions. Generally speaking, all four women exhibit remarkably similar aspirations and failings, in that each attempts to impose on life a romantic ideal, which crumbles after a series of confrontations with reality. These women are victims not only of the tensions between the public world and the private world of their creative imaginations, but also of their own emotional and intellectual limitations, some of which are the result of their having 'internalised' the values of their society. One could say of them, as Matthew Arnold said of the Romantic poets, that they just 'did not know enough'. If the fidelity of the provincial heroine to her creative vision gives her intensity and grandeur, her blindness to the real world also makes her frequently unpleasant. Each of these romantic heroines is therefore dissected by the irony of her realist–creator. None the less, each author retains a certain admiration for his character's attempts to arrange human lives as though they were only materials for art, and, in fact, each identifies to a degree with her. Flaubert said, 'I *am* Madame Bovary', and Jane Austen warns us that Emma is a 'heroine whom no one but myself will much like'. Dorothea Brooke has often been interpreted, notably by F. R. Leavis, as a dream picture of George Eliot as she would have liked to be.

The *données* of the predicament in which all four heroines find – or lose – themselves can be classified as geographical or spatial, social, educational and sexual. Of these four factors which give shape to the heroines' aspirations, as well as restricting them, the last is the most crucial, since it determines the particular form assumed by the other three. The final and inescapable prison for all four women is neither the provinces, nor marriage, nor ignorance, but the prison of womanhood. Henry James felt that all Americans were provincials in contrast to their European cousins. Similarly, all women remain provincials in relation to masculine culture with its varied options and outlets.

Since the eighteenth century two principal types of fictional
heroines have both reflected and shaped social attitudes. A brief
poem by Emily Dickinson, a real-life 'provincial heroine', pinpoints
the characteristic dilemma of all those women in fiction whom we
shall designate as 'Emma's Daughters', to distinguish them from
the very different 'Pamela's Daughters':

> I took my power in my Hand –
> And went against the World –
> 'Twas not so much as David – had –
> But I – was twice as bold –
> I aimed my Pebble – but myself
> Was all the one that fell –
> Was it Goliath – was too large –
> Or was myself – too small?[3]

Specifically, Miss Dickinson exposes the paradox with which all of
them might well be concerned – were they able to locate and
verbalise the underlying causes for the failure of their aspirations:
the relationship between personal limitations and the barriers
erected against individual fulfilment by society.

The opposition between Pamela's daughters, defined by R. P.
Utter and G. B. Needham,[4] and Emma's is extremely significant, for
these two striking alternatives have represented what are probably
the strongest currents of influence on the realistic portrayal of
feminine psychology in prose fiction – and on the formulation of real
feminine aspirations. Briefly, the 'Emma'-heroine is isolated, gifted
and imaginative; she displays energy and initiative in her attempts
to mould external reality by means of her imaginative creativity. In
real life, Emily Dickinson found a creative outlet in her verse; but the
fictional 'Emma'-heroine is often sadly inarticulate, frustrated by
her failure to find any worthy outlet.

The 'Pamela'-heroine, however, who has been studied by Utter
and Needham and hailed by Ian Watt as 'a new, fully developed and
immensely influential stereotype of the feminine role', is always
'very young, very inexperienced and so delicate in physical and
mental constitution that she faints at any sexual advance; essentially
passive, she is devoid of any feelings towards her admirer until the
marriage knot is tied.'[5] One can imagine how repugnant Emma, for
instance, would find Pamela's 'lucky knack of fits'. Moreover,
however inexperienced, the 'Emma'-heroine, with the possible
exception of the puzzling Isabel Archer, is womanly rather than
girlish; and a chief source of conflict in the plot is invariably her

recognition of a passionate attachment to a man with whom she fears or knows marriage will be impossible.

Ian Watt suggests that the emergence of the 'Pamela'-type is closely related to the rise of the novel itself, which occurred in a period dominated by economic individualism and the Puritan ethos. It was an era when women learned to rise socially through marriage, and when they increasingly assumed the functions of mere sexual objects or decorative status symbols for their husbands. One can easily understand the appeal of *Pamela* or *Clarissa* to female readers, themselves more and more forced to speculate on questions of courtship and social betterment through marriage, of finding a new role for women, and of reconciling love and marriage. In other words, Pamela's problem is not so very different, after all, from that of the conspicuously unvirtuous Moll Flanders. Even Clarissa falls into this category of socially ambitious heroines because she aspires to marry an aristocrat – after first reforming him! The Emma–Dorothea–Isabel-heroine, on the other hand, free from economic necessity, is able to choose as she sees fit – even, as she sometimes wishes, to choose spinsterhood – to dream about subjects other than her own social betterment and a conventional fulfilment, and to be much less materially dependent on others in creating her own fate and conditions.

Both traditions stress the important, and sometimes dominant, role a woman can play in society. The power of the 'Pamela'-heroine is, however, based on her very 'femininity', her appealing mixture of helplessness and moral rectitude, whereas the 'Emma'-heroine prides herself (often mistakenly) on her autonomy, her self-determination. She considers herself (again, often mistakenly) to be much less wrapped in the social fabric than her 'Pamela'-sisters because either her position is so secure or her education so unusually full that she can consider herself superior to her surroundings.

Any 'external' evidence of influence among the four authors who created variations on the 'Emma' theme is less persuasive than the internal evidence of the texts of their novels, in which even minor details of plot and imagery are repeated.

In the first place, all four novels are concerned with the interaction – or lack of it – between their heroines and the public world of provincial society. In each novel the sense of a new order – the rising wealthy middle class in *Emma*, the Reform Bill in *Middlemarch*, the much talked-about but badly demonstrated scientific progress of

Madame Bovary, the conservative radicalism of England in *Portrait* – has a subtle yet vital relation to the position of women. The 'frail vessels of affection', it would seem, remain victims of a 'culture lag', hazily aware of exciting expansions in the world about them, but excluded from full participation in these activities by virtue of their womanhood.

A critique of marriage, the only social role permitted women, is therefore a major concern in each of these novels. It is surely no coincidence that Emma Woodhouse and Isabel Archer seek outlets other than marriage, and that Emma displays a marked scorn for the taste of men who, she thinks, would all normally prefer a Harriet Smith to herself. Emma uses Harriet as a support in her attack against the masculine judgement, which in her opinion loves appearance alone, whereas she sees her *own* character as a triumph of brains over beauty: 'till it appears that men are much more philosophic on the subject of beauty than they are generally supposed; till they do fall in love with well-informed minds instead of handsome faces, a girl, with such loveliness as Harriet, has a certainty of being admired and sought after'.[6] If Dorothea intends from the very beginning to marry, it is only in order to help inspire a latter-day Hooker, Pascal or Milton, since there is nothing she can accomplish alone. Or, as one of George Eliot's chapter epigraphs concedes:

> Since I can do no good because a woman,
> Reach constantly at something that is near it.
> (Beaumont and Fletcher, *The Maid's Tragedy*)

All three reject, or at least intend to reject, romantic love. Emma Bovary, on the other hand, accepts marriage in the first place because she expects to find in it the poetry and colour of a Scott novel; when this fails, she loses little time in finding a means of self-expression far beyond the limits of the marriage bond.

All four envision a role somehow nobler or more original than domesticity and the rearing of children. Emma Bovary is completely indifferent to the child, Berthe, except when it suits her purpose to use her as an excuse. Isabel loses her child by Osmond, for this is a marriage doomed to barrenness; but there is poetic justice in the fact that she becomes more of a mother to Pansy than Madame Merle can ever be. Emma Woodhouse and Dorothea decide early that they will forgo childbearing and that their estates will therefore pass on to their nephews, but soon forget the very existence of the latter when they begin to plan families of their own. The romantic love at first rejected by both Isabel and Dorothea is personified by Caspar Goodwood and Will Ladislaw. Isabel's and Dorothea's first discovery of physical passion occurs in almost identical scenes. Isabel's lightning-flash perception of the physical being of Caspar Goodwood, which convinces her to resume a fate altogether different from that she would share with him, is similar in technique but opposite in result to the scene in which Dorothea finally yields to her love for Will during a thunderstorm. The eventual fate of all four women, however, is marriage, whether or not it is occasioned by romantic love or meets with the author's approval.

The tragic proportions of *Middlemarch* and *The Portrait of a Lady*, of which both authors frequently remind us, are derived largely from the implied constrast between Isabel's and Dorothea's awareness of large conceptions, such as the feminist movement, philanthropy and art, outside the provincial domain, and the domestic role allotted to them within it. If the failure lies in a distinctive brand of 'egoism' within the heroine on the one hand, on the other it lies in the pettiness of her immediate surroundings, by which she is 'cabined, cribb'd, confined'.

If such are the similarities of the heroines' respective societies, and of the roles they are allowed to play in them, the resemblances between their individual portraits are even more striking. In each novel there is, in fact, a revealing 'Portrait of a Lady', and each author seeks to draw an analogy between his art and that of the painter as a means to the end of permitting us to see his heroine steadily and see her whole. James's is completely verbal, the novelist's equivalent for the pictures in the Touchetts' gallery. In the other three, however, the word 'portrait' can be used in its literal sense. While she is in Rome on her honeymoon, Dorothea is painted as a saint by Naumann, Will Ladislaw's artist friend. Her husband, the pedantic Edward Casaubon, ironically, is represented as Saint Thomas Aquinas, 'in a disputation too abstract to be represented, but listened to with more or less attention by an audience above'.[7] The entire Roman scene, in fact, is so close in purpose and method to James's description of Isabel Archer's stay in Rome that one is tempted to see in it the nucleus of inspiration for James's entire *Portrait*.

Emma Woodhouse is the only one of the heroines to have the dubious distinction of painting her own portrait, a deed that is delightfully in character for this female artist in matchmaking.

Actually, the portrait she paints, in her dilettantish fashion, is of Harriet Smith; but her idealisation of Harriet, to whom she attributed her own tall figure and elegance, as the perceptive Mr Knightley immediately remarks – as well as, we may suspect from the dialogue, her eyebrows and lashes – results in a self-portrait more revealing than any direct physical description Miss Austen gives of her.

There is no full-scale portrait of Emma Bovary, only a miniature, which is perhaps in keeping with the unheroic, sordid picture Flaubert gives us of her. She has presented this miniature to Rodolphe Boulanger, who in turn treats her as if she had no more life or feeling than her picture, which he jumbles up in a box, together with her love letters, mixing them like so much trash with his souvenirs of other cast-off mistresses.

All four novelists transcend the analogy to painting in their verbal portraiture, for the heroines' physical beauty is a herald of what Emma Woodhouse would call their 'inner resources'. Their creators move back and forth skilfully between outward appearances and fantasising, often tormented, psyches. Jane Austen immediately tells us that Emma Woodhouse is 'handsome, clever, and rich'. These traits are shared by three of our heroines; the exception is Emma Bovary, beautiful enough to impress even the jaded Rodolphe, but poor rather than rich, imaginative rather than clever. These last two qualities create her tragedy, since she yearns for romance and luxury, but lacks the critical judgement to cope with the realities of her character and surroundings. Beauty, wealth and intelligence – if we may be permitted to alter Miss Austen's phrase in order to leave the most crucial for last – provide us with pegs on which to hang these radical nineteenth-century reassessments of the feminine potential.

Not only are all four women 'handsome', they even possess many of the same physical characteristics. Their type of beauty, however, runs counter to the expectations of their age concerning the *jeune fille* or ingenue. All are brunettes, generally dark- or grey-eyed, except for Emma Bovary, whose dark blue eyes have a certain symbolic significance in the novel. Usually blonde hair and blue eyes are reserved for the heroine's foils, a pretty little nitwit like Harriet Smith, or a calculating, beautiful nitwit like Rosamond Vincy. Nor is the blonde–brunette contrast altogether due to the Scott romance, as Alexander Welsh supposes, from the example of Rebecca and Rowena, since Miss Austen is already using it in 1816.[8] One would have more justification in theorising that the authors' distaste or contempt for blondes is the result of their satirical view of courtly love and its sentimentally idealised lady, invariably a grey- or blue-eyed blonde in constant need of rescue. In that case the brunette, who shares the fate of the vast majority of women, could be a projection of her creator's realistic interests. Whatever the reason, the pattern reverses the usual romantic tendency to render the blonde as innocence personified, and the brunette as mysterious or sinister.

In addition to their colouring, three of the four share the trait of queenliness or statuesqueness. Again Emma Bovary is the exception, a small woman. But then Flaubert aimed at dissecting and destroying all of Emma's vanity and illusions, while James, Austen and Eliot intended to retain the reader's admiration for their heroines. Their height is a clue to the bursting health and vitality of Emma, Isabel and Dorothea, all of whom are extremely fond of long walks in the country. Emma's health is in sharp contrast to the general sickliness of her father, Harriet and Jane Fairfax; but Emma is forced to live within her father's private world of ill health or hypochondria which shapes his well-meaning attempts to interpret everyone else's life. The freedom-loving Dorothea, who we are told is also passionately susceptible to the sensuous delights of horseback riding, suffers much the same fate as Emma in her marriage to the sickly Mr Casaubon, for she is walled up with him in *his* private labyrinth of sickly scholarship. Isabel Archer's good health prevents her from entering into the most meaningful relationship with the tubercular Ralph Touchett; though it is his ill health and his father's, together with their delight in passive observation of humanity, that create Isabel's opportunity for wealth, freedom and experience. The result, however, her marriage to Gilbert Osmond, falls far short of Ralph's expectations. As the reader sees Isabel walking in the Campagna with her stepdaughter, he is told that although her stride is long and elastic, compared to poor little Pansy's, it is not so long or so springy as it was before her marriage.

Although Emma Bovary is subject to all sorts of *crises de nerfs*, doubtless hysterical or psychosomatic, much is made also of her physical energy and fervid womanliness once the frustrations of married life are assuaged by Rodolphe. Their meetings take place outdoors, in her garden or in the woods, and the liaison is begun through his offering her the use of a horse, supposedly to remedy her ill health. Like the other heroines, she loves to walk, as well as ride; but her long early-morning walks into the country have as their objective Rodolphe's farm. These walks are ironically paralleled by her self-prostituting wanderings at the end of the novel. When she is most corrupted by Rodolphe, she even adopts a certain masculinity in her style of dress and begins to smoke cigars. She assumes that only men are free, and that her sole release from both the prison of habit and the prison of womanhood can come by means of living vicariously through a son:

> Un homme, au moins, est libre; il peut parcourir les passions et les pays, traverser les obstacles, mordre aux bonheurs les plus lointains. Mais une femme est empêchée continuellement. Inerte et flexible à la fois, elle a contre elle les mollesses de la chair avec les dépendances de la loi. Sa volonté, comme le voile de son chapeau retenu par un cordon, palpite à tous les vents.[9]

Although she would not recognise it as such, she is making, in her speech as in her dress, the nucleus of a feminist protest against the alternately passive–responsive role imposed on women both by society and by their own emotional vulnerability. Her key simile, however, which compares the feminine will to the veil of a lady's hat, betrays the ineffectiveness of the rebellion on both the physical and spiritual levels.

It is revealing that the other three women are themselves little aware of their handsomeness, a fact demonstrated by their elegant simplicity of dress, in contrast to the fripperies and petty vanity of Harriet or especially Rosamond. Except for Madame Bovary, none of them errs on the side of personal vanity. Yet each is described by the admiring hero as an angel, saint or madonna. Only the realistic Mr Knightley refrains from such rhapsodising; and Emma Bovary is seen as an angel or madonna by her husband and her lover when she is most 'rolling in the dust', as James put it.[10]

That Emma Woodhouse, Dorothea and Isabel are rich as well as handsome is a determining factor in their fates. Emma and Dorothea are isolated by wealth and social position from the townspeople, and the failure to empathise which both demonstrate early in the novels is largely a result of this isolation. Isabel, on the other hand, receives her money comparatively late; but it raises her into a social sphere in which she can fall prey to Gilbert Osmond, so that she is forced to live in some aesthetic, inverted 'paradise' instead of contributing to the mainstream of human life. Emma Bovary's relative poverty demonstrates that her economic situation – in reverse – is as influential in her destiny as in that of the three heiresses. Père Rouault has evidently suffered from a decline in fortune after giving his daughter a convent education superior to her class, and is willing to accept the first suitor for Emma who is not exigent about a substantial dowry.

The third, and most important, trait the heroines share is 'cleverness' – or, in the case of Emma Bovary, a 'romantic imagination' and an education beyond the level of her class. One of the immediate results of this cleverness, as of their wealth, is the isolation it imposes on them. In the first place, all four lack either a mother or both parents, and as Jane Austen explains about Emma, the absence of a mother's authority over a clever, imaginative girl can easily result in a tendency to think too well of herself, and in a play of the mind which becomes a little too free. The simple farmer, Père Rouault, the semi-invalid Mr Woodhouse, the dabbler Mr Brooke, all so limited themselves, can do nothing but indulge in uncritical praise – in Brooke's case, 'up to a point, you know' – of their daughters' or nieces' comparative brilliance. In addition, Dorothea, Emma and Isabel all have sisters as limited as the parent or guardian, and the reputation of being the clever one in the family may also result in their creation of a somewhat self-centred universe.

References to houses and property, both literal and figurative, reflect the heroines' wealth and provide raw materials for their creative imaginations. At times the imagery of architecture and property invests their dreams with an objective reality, but at other times it reinforces our sense of their social isolation and virtual imprisonment. Much of the action of each novel turns upon a contrast between an almost idealised setting on the one hand, and vulgar ostentation or a luxurious dungeon on the other. Thus the hymn to the 'Englishness' and gentility of Donwell Abbey and Hartfield is contrasted to the Sucklings' pretentious Maple Grove; the freedom and airiness of Freshitt (freshet?) and Tipton are compared to Mr Casaubon's locked in Lowick (low wick?), with its poisonous yew-tree walk in which he dies; and the serenity and 'Englishness' of Gardencourt are compared to the barren Roccanera (black rock) in which Isabel is imprisoned by Osmond.

A house is a concrete manifestation of a certain society and way of life, and these are, after all, novels of manners. But more important, a house is also a projection of a certain individual consciousness, and can thereby symbolise its inhabitant's soul even more effectively than portraiture. James sets forth the architectural analogy of a 'house of fiction' in his 'Preface' to *The Portrait of a Lady*. This house of fiction becomes, within the novel, the symbol for the 'structure' erected by Isabel's own consciousness. Her consciousness, moreover, pieces together the realities of human existence in a series of houses beginning with the old home in Albany where, by shutting out the street, she was able to make of the study itself merely the visible embodiment of her own imagination. Her expansive 'architecture of consciousness' is contrasted to Osmond's mean, petty soul, which is described by James as though it were the interior of a house in which Isabel is being stifled: 'It was the house of darkness, the house of dumbness, the house of suffocation. Osmond's beautiful mind gave it neither light nor air; Osmond's beautiful mind indeed seemed to peep down from a small high window and mock at her' (*Portrait*, p. 353).

Not too surprisingly, George Eliot's edifice could also be called a house of fiction; not only is the heroine seen in relation to the houses in which she is free and enslaved, but also Casaubon's mind, in particular, is likened to a musty closed structure with no windows on the outside. Like Isabel, Dorothea finds that 'the large vistas and wide fresh air which she had dreamed of finding in her husband's mind were replaced by anterooms and winding passages which seemed to lead nowhere' (*Middlemarch*, p. 145). Her own creative intelligence also resembles Isabel's in its impulse towards 'architecture', but Dorothea's ambitions are more pragmatic than the American girl's. She desires to justify her existence by renovating cottages and beautifying the lives of the poor, for which Caleb Garth pays her the compliment of seeing in her a man's sense.

The imagination by which each heroine tries to transform her own life and the lives of those around her owes a great debt to the Quixote tradition. Each girl is raised in isolation, lacks practical experience and has a knowledge of life derived solely from books, supplemented by her own fantasies. Harry Levin quotes Soren Kierkegaard, who complained around 1843 of the European failure to exploit the possibilities of a 'female Quixote': 'It is remarkable that the whole of European literature lacks a feminine counterpart to *Don Quixote*. May not the time for this be coming, may not the continent of sentimentality yet be discovered?'[11] Levin himself goes on to make an interesting comment on this task suggested by Kierkegaard, indicating that it was finally accomplished by Flaubert: 'To set forth what Kierkegaard had spied out, to invade the continent of sentimentality, to create a female Quixote – mock-romantic where Cervantes had been mock-heroic – was a man's job. Jane Austen might have done it, but not George Sand.'[12] Actually, of course, Jane Austen had already done it, and not in 1843, but in 1816. Moreover, she followed a path laid out by Charlotte Ramsey Lennox's feminised version of Cervantes's novel, *The Female Quixote* (1752), a satire about the damaging effect on a young girl of reading French romances of the Scudéry variety.[13]

Anthony Thorlby has based a fairly extended comparison of *Don Quixote* and *Madame Bovary* on Flaubert's tremendous admiration for Cervantes: 'Don Quixote is misled by his imagination, Emma by her feelings. In the case of Cervantes the contrast is between the real and the ideal, in the case of Flaubert it is between reality and sentiment.'[14] Finally, George Eliot uses the episode of Mambrino's helmet as one of her chapter headings in *Middlemarch* to point up the discrepancies in vision between Dorothea and Celia, her Sancho Panza-like 'unenthusiastic sister' whose 'blonde flesh' suffers much under Dorothea's transcendental longings.

All four novels are concerned with the developing consciousness of their heroines, or rather, in the case of Madame Bovary, with its failure to develop. All emphasise, at any rate, the need for critical judgement and a growing perception of reality to replace Quixotism. With Emma, Dorothea and Isabel one source of the 'shock of recognition' is the perception of a previously misunderstood relation between two other characters.

Quixotism frequently assumes the form of religious or philosophical idealism in all but Emma Woodhouse, who very practically sets about matchmaking. As many of Isabel's aspirations are transcendental, Emma Bovary's and Dorothea Brooke's are religious and mystical. This idealism tends to shut out reality from Isabel, locked in her study, and from the dim-sighted Dorothea, so that in both there is a failure of perception. Isabel's Emersonian expectations – Osmond likens her to a Unitarian preacher – probably echo her creator's sometime interests, just as Dorothea's reading of Jeremy Taylor and Pascal echoes Eliot's period of higher criticism, which she subsequently rejected for novel writing.

For most readers, even such dim-sighted idealism is infinitely preferable to Rosamond Vincy's tatting and piano-playing, although the latter are more in accord with the nineteenth century's generally accepted definition of the 'accomplished young lady'.

Each novelist takes satirical aim at this feminine stereotype by using the same device: depicting the amusing vicissitudes of a piano. Emma is envious of Jane Fairfax's skill, and a piano forms the basis for her wild imagining about some intrigue between Jane and Mr Dixon. Emma Bovary, who also has the convent or finishing-school accomplishments, uses piano lessons as an excuse to go to Rouen and meet Léon. Dorothea, needless to say, scorns such a useless skill, in contrast to Rosamond; and Isabel at first mistakes Madame Merle's technical skill as a pianist for culture and greatness of soul. There is, in other words, a tendency for each author to point to the idiocies of women's education as a justification for his heroine's ardent attempts to find some more widely applicable concept of human existence. The feebleness of education also explains why each girl, brought in contact with great art or religion or the grandeur of the past and seen in relation to it, fails to comprehend that it may have any personal meaning for her. Emma Bovary in the great cathedral at Rouen, Dorothea and Isabel in Rome, remain oblivious to deeper meanings. Emma is conscious only of her own adulterous desires; Dorothea of her inability to appreciate beauty denied to the masses; Isabel, of her own problems and fear of free choice.

The awareness of their own deficiencies, or simply a vague longing for beauty, leaves each either a prey or a suitable mate for a dilettante, whom she naturally sees as a hero–teacher. Gilbert Osmond, in whom Isabel sees total sufficiency as an artist of life, the superficial Léon, the versatile Will Ladislaw, all fit into this category, and only Will comes off well. Emma's only leaning toward a dilettantish male is her imagined interest in the foppish Frank Churchill. But she herself is a perfect dilettante in painting, music and literature, and Frank shares many of her qualities.

One of the most conspicuous signs of the reformed 'Female Quixote' is the aversion she takes to books. Once in contact with reality, both Isabel and Dorothea find that they are reading only 'words, words, words'; and Emma Bovary loses her passionate empathy with Scott's heroine in *Lucia di Lammermoor* when she meets Léon at the opera. Another amusing sign is that three of the heroines gradually develop a sense of humour as their perception is sharpened in the course of the narrative. Emma Bovary, needless to say, might have been saved by a corresponding cultivation of wit and wisdom. Emma Woodhouse develops the ability to laugh at herself rather than at others – incidentally one of the reasons why the reader does not dislike her, as Miss Austen pessimistically predicted. Dorothea's humour is subordinate to her earnestness, but she is finally equal to Celia's undercutting and is able to indulge in a little gentle laughter at her sister's limitations. Most conspicuously, Isabel, humourless before her marriage, rapidly acquires a barbed wit verging on sarcasm.

These are just a few of the complex interrelations among the novels; but to avoid Casaubon's mistake of detecting analogies which were not 'tested by the necessity of forming anything which had sharper collisions than an elaborate notion of Gog and Magog' (*Middlemarch*, p. 351), it is well to remember that the differences are just as important as the similarities. This study is not, after all, directed towards demonstrating an identity of inspiration in all four novels, but rather towards tracing the same theme as it develops in different periods, conditions and settings. There are important differences between English, French and American provincial societies and in the authors' attitudes towards them, most clearly demonstrated by the women's varied cultural outlets: matchmaking for Emma, adultery for Madame Bovary, social concern in Dorothea Brooke, the development of an 'architecture of consciousness' in Isabel Archer. However varied the outlets may be, nevertheless, determined as they are by four rather different cultures, backgrounds and temperaments, the one overriding similarity in the four novels is the nature of their heroines' original creative and romantic aspirations, and of their often misguided attempts to impart form and beauty to the mediocrity of the life surrounding them. In this, all four are *artistes manqués*, frustrated both by the provincial setting and by their own limitations of education, taste or character.

It is curious that, of the four heroines, it is the two created by male novelists whose fates seem most unresolved or unconvincing. Emma Bovary dies hard; and after her death, her influence on Charles persists, so that Flaubert must finally destroy him too to conform with the rigorous pessimism of the rest of the novel. In a sense, Isabel's zest for life also dies hard when she elects to return to Osmond. Neither the creator nor the reader feels ultimately satisfied that the fate James depicts could, realistically, be that bleak and absolute. It has often been remarked that both Flaubert and James give evidence of possessing themselves what is described (perhaps mistakenly) as a 'feminine' sensibility; perhaps it is this side of their own creative imaginations which 'dies hard' in their heroines.

The two women novelists, Jane Austen and George Eliot, seem not to suffer from such an ambivalence in depicting their heroines' ultimate fates; both regard their creations objectively and recognise, in practice as well as in theory, that 'the whole of anything is never told',[15] that Emma Woodhouse will never be entirely tamed and domesticated by Mr Knightley, that she will continue to misdirect her creativity toward matchmaking; that Dorothea *could* have done something better had she (and her surroundings) been something better, that what we see is only the fragment of a life which is *not* completed, for better or for worse, by marriage to Will Ladislaw.

In all four novels, however, we are left with an acute sense of the extent to which 'a man's [or woman's] reach must exceed his grasp', and with a realisation of why such a novel can provide an appropriate vehicle for the analysis of the forces, both internal and external, which align themselves against the workings of the feminine creative imagination. The 'literary space' which the four novelists leave to the reader is a function of their heroines' infinite, unsatisfied aspirations, and confirms our feelings that all four novels 'burst, with a latent extravagance, [their] mould'.[16]

As we have seen, a literary tradition dealing with feminine provincial creativity began to crystallise and define itself even before the time of Jane Austen. And if the provinces themselves have almost disappeared since the days of Theodore Dreiser's *Sister Carrie*, H. G. Wells's *Ann Veronica* and Sinclair Lewis's *Main Street*, James points the way to novels dealing with feminine creativity stifled by a provincialism of both the mind and background. But the four novels studied here seem to present the dilemma of feminine isolation and creativity with a fullness not elsewhere attained, and their heroines capture the imagination of the reader to such an extent that they have almost become archetypal figures.

2

Emma Woodhouse: Self-portrait of a Lady

I took my power in my Hand –
And went against the World –
'Twas not so much as David – had –
But I – was twice as bold –
I aimed my Pebble – but Myself
Was all the one that fell –
Was it Goliath – was too large –
Or was myself – too small?
(Emily Dickinson, *c*. 1862)

In *The Portrait of a Lady*, Henry James cautions his reader to regard Isabel Archer not with 'scientific detachment', but with tenderness.[1] By the same token, Jane Austen warns the readers of *Emma* that she fears she has created 'a heroine whom no one but myself will much like'.[2] Both authors are aware that their heroines' ill-conceived and worse-executed romantic aspirations may arouse feelings of deep-seated hostility in their audience. It is probable that their uneasiness about the reader's reaction to their protagonists stems from the symbiotic relationship between their own imaginative sensibilities and those of the heroines as artist figures.

Jane Austen's Emma can, in fact, be seen as the prototype of a distinguished line of heroines who are active shaping forces in their fictional worlds rather than passive victims in the tradition of Samuel Richardson's Pamela and Clarissa, or muses and sources of inspiration for male artists and artist figures. I have referred to this lineage – which includes, most notably, George Eliot's Dorothea Brooke and, with some slight modification, Flaubert's Emma Bovary, in addition to Emma Woodhouse and Isabel Archer – as 'Emma's Daughters', in contradistinction to the very different 'Pamela's Daughters' defined by Utter and Needham.[3]

Of the four active, imaginative and usually misguided female artist figures, only Emma Woodhouse attempts, not merely to shape life as if it were art, but also to give it concrete aesthetic

18

embodiment in verbal games and charades, drawings and sketches, music and dancing. Emma's portrait of her little protégée, Harriet Smith, serves as a distillation of all Emma's creative strengths and shortcomings.[4] But before we examine the portrait itself, it would be well to assess the clues we are given as to the quality of the mind that produces it.

JANE AUSTEN'S HOUSE OF FICTION: THE RHYTHM OF EXPANSION AND CONTRACTION

In no other of Jane Austen's novels is the focus so exclusively on the consciousness of the protagonist as it is in *Emma*. From the opening paragraph, Emma's strong personality dominates:

> Emma Woodhouse, handsome, clever, and rich, with a comfortable home and happy disposition, seemed to unite some of the best blessings of existence; and had lived nearly twenty-one years in the world with very little to distress or vex her. ...
> The real evils indeed of Emma's situation were the power of having rather too much her own way, and a disposition to think a little too well of herself.[5]

Despite Austen's misgivings, most readers share the same interest in Emma's growth towards awareness as Mr Knightley: 'There is an anxiety, a curiosity in what one feels for Emma. I wonder what will become of her!' (p. 29).

Emma's dominance is surprising in that she is, in a geographical sense, the most provincial of heroines. Her final awareness is not based on any breadth of travel, for she never leaves Highbury and rarely leaves the seclusion of Hartfield. The very first chapter of the novel creates in the reader an initial sympathy for Emma which can never be completely destroyed. It presents the private world of Hartfield, which is cut off from even Highbury itself by virtue of Mr Woodhouse's valetudinarianism, the Woodhouses' social position and the complete lack of any intellectual stimulation for Emma. Hartfield is the architectural embodiment (probably signalled also by Emma's last name, 'Woodhouse') of what Mr Woodhouse calls 'one's family circle', which the reader recognises as a form of spatial and spiritual entrapment for Emma.

In certain crucial respects even Jane Fairfax's relative poverty has permitted her a greater freedom and breadth of vision than Emma's socially secure but isolated position. Jane's feelings were awakened to maturity when she met Frank Churchill at Weymouth, a celebrated watering-place. Emma, however, has never seen the sea (p. 78), and it is almost a full year after Jane is secretly engaged to Frank that Emma becomes fully conscious of her passion for Mr Knightley.[6] We learn afterwards that Frank and Jane met at Weymouth in October, while Emma, Mr Knightley and Mr Woodhouse were coincidentally attending the wedding of Miss Taylor, Emma's ex-governess, and Mr Weston, Frank's father. Thus both Jane and Emma are in a sense launched into the world at the same time, Jane without the protection of the Campbells once Miss Campbell marries Mr Dixon, Emma without the indulgent care of Miss Taylor. The consequences of these two events, so apparently unrelated but both triggered by a marriage, subsequently are to become intertwined at Highbury.

Not only has Emma never seen the sea, but she has never even visited Box Hill in her own neighbourhood. Emma's isolation is typified by the early scene in which, returning from a Christmas visit to Randalls, the Westons' house, in a closed carriage and trapped by the snowy weather, she is forced to listen to the absurd, pompous proposal of Mr Elton. On a less comic level, we are reminded of the scene in Flaubert's novel when we witness Emma Bovary's entrapment in a liaison with Léon Dupuis, which is commenced in a closed carriage hurtling blindly and uncontrollably through the streets of Rouen. However abrasive or embarrassing the characters' mutual relations in *Emma*, there is no escape from the variety of emotions bottled up in a provincial town: 'Not one of them had the power of removal, or of effecting any material change of society. They must encounter each other, and make the best of it' (p. 110).

It is no accident that Jane Austen has chosen her most restricted setting as the background for her most ambitious and concentrated study of a single heroine. This is the one Austen novel, moreover, which takes as its title the heroine's name.[7] *Emma* would seem to be her favourite character study, whereas *Sense and Sensibility* and *Pride and Prejudice*, as their titles indicate, point to the defining and refining in concrete terms of certain abstract Johnsonian principles of morality and conduct. *Emma* was intended as Jane Austen's ultimate step in critical realism – gone are the travels of Elizabeth

Bennet, the melodramatic elopement of Lydia Bennet and Wick-ham. One could say that in *Emma*, Jane Austen has anticipated Gustave Flaubert's ambition to write 'un livre sur rien'. Nothing matters in the novel except Emma and a whole series of foils, reflectors and interpreters of her character: Mr Knightley, Mrs Elton, Mrs Weston, Miss Bates, Frank Churchill, Jane Fairfax, Harriet Smith, Mr Woodhouse.

Emma's background has failed to provide her with a frame of reference against which she can set the advantages and frustrations of provincial life. Like Mrs Lennox's Arabella, she has had to invent her own frame, drawing upon materials supplied by her reading and her fancy. Her attempts to organise the lives of others according to some aesthetically pleasing formulation seem ultimately directed towards an assertion of her own power and integrity as a would-be artist. What she fails to recognise, however, is that such an endeavour presupposes knowledge of the social structure sur-rounding her, as well as of the personalities involved.

Despite all the limitations on Emma's knowledge and judgement, *Emma* is a *Bildungsroman*, and the most provincial of settings can give rise to universal considerations. As Saintsbury said of Austen, 'If her world is a microcosm ... the cosmic quality of it is at least as eminent as the littleness.'[8] Although it would be difficult to support any contention that Highbury by itself constitutes a microcosm of English life, it does become one with the addition of certain newcomers, or comparative newcomers, to the town – Mr Weston, Jane Fairfax, Frank Churchill, Mrs Elton. The reader is permitted, along with Emma, a vision of the world outside Highbury by virtue of the fact that the world comes to Highbury. One is intensely aware throughout the novel of what could be called 'the romance of newcomers'. The 'entrances and exits' of the various characters impart to the novel its rhythm of expansion and contraction. Even the fact of having left Highbury temporarily and returning is enough to make one the centre of attention for the entire town. Mr Weston, incurring the righteous indignation of John Knightley, hurries along to Hartfield after a day of business in London, 'cheerful as usual, and with all the right of being principal talker, which a day spent any where from home confers' (p. 235). How much stronger, then, is the claim to attention of the real newcomers to Highbury society: Jane, Frank and Mrs Elton. In addition, there are frequent allusions to the world outside Highbury which permit Jane Austen to range geographically all over England and Ireland without ever moving her protagonist away from home. As Mary Lascelles astutely observes, never before had Jane Austen used so many 'offstage' characters as in *Emma*, people whom we never really meet, yet who play a principal role in the drama, ranging from Mr Knightley's right-hand man, William Larkins, to Colonel Campbell and his wife, the Dixons in Ireland, the Churchills at Enscombe, and last but not least, the Sucklings at Maple Grove.[9] Jane Austen has managed by these means to retain the unities of time, place and action of a classical drama; and at the same time to transport the reader outside Highbury while unravelling simultaneously two or three separate threads of plot.

As John Knightley remarks to Emma at one point, 'Your neighbourhood is increasing and you mix more with it' (pp. 242–3).[10] The first three chapters of the novel introduce all three of its major worlds or circles which are to enlarge Emma's own 'circle of consciousness'. From Chapter One, which presents Mr Woodhouse's 'family circle' at Hartfield, we move in Chapter Two to Mr Weston, who has just broken up Mr Woodhouse's circle by marrying Miss Taylor. Mr Weston affords us our first glimpse of Frank Churchill in his conversation, thus presenting the macrocosm, or world outside Highbury, in the shape of Enscombe and London, where Mr Weston meets his son every year. Chapter Three introduces Highbury itself, delineated in detail in all its almost static social structure, which provides the principal stage for the action of the novel.

As the novel progresses, these three worlds increasingly intermingle or collide. Emma is hurried with increasing rapidity out of her musings by the social demands made on her. Her consciousness barely assimilates one discovery before another crowds into its place, leaving her little time for repentance. By the end of the novel, she has barely begun to worry over Frank Churchill's supposed disappointment of Harriet when Harriet reveals that her real interest is not in Frank at all, but in Mr Knightley, and Emma's sudden recognition of her own love for Mr Knightley banishes all other concerns.

'Woman's Destiny': the Marriage Market

Emma's matchmaking schemes for Harriet can be seen as a product of her provincial plight; lacking sufficient outlets for the free play of her imagination, she romanticises what objects she *does* have in view. The particular form her imaginings take, however, also suggests certain feminist presentiments in the novel. Since the role of women is so completely enmeshed in the social pattern, Emma attempts to rearrange that pattern to suit her own ends. But her choice of subject matter – marriage – reveals that she can never free her spirit entirely from the traditional, socially sanctioned role of woman. For a time, at least, Emma entertains delusive hopes that, although her imagination may be dependent on materials drawn from matchmaking, she herself can remain free. She boasts to Harriet of the 'resources' which will make marriage unnecessary for her:

> If I know myself, Harriet, mine is an active, busy mind, with a great many independent resources; and I do not perceive why I should be more in want of employment at forty or fifty than one-and-twenty. ... If I draw less, I shall read more; if I give up music, I shall take to carpet-work. And as for objects of interest, objects for the affections, which is in truth the great point of inferiority the want of which is really the great evil to be avoided in *not* marrying, I shall be very well off, with all the children of a sister I love so much, to care about. There will be enough of them, in all probability, to supply every sort of sensation that declining life can need ... and though my attachment to none can equal that of a parent, it suits my ideas of comfort better than what is warmer and blinder.   (p. 66)[11]

If this passage did not provide sufficient ironic commentary on itself, later on Mrs Elton makes much the same boast about her spinster days: 'Blessed with so many resources within myself, the world was not necessary to me' (p. 213).

Emma reveals in her statements a great many truths without being really 'acquainted with' herself at all. Several critics (Duffy, Wilson, Mudrick) consider her distaste for 'what is warmer and blinder' to be rooted in a fear of sexual passion. She is probably, however, only echoing her father's idea of 'comfort' and her own knowledge that her situation with him will in any event preclude marriage. Nor is there any young man in Highbury who would be deemed suitable for her.

Emma says, 'I have none of the usual inducements of women to marry', and proceeds to name them: 'Fortune I do not want; employment I do not want; consequence I do not want; I believe few married women are half as much mistress of their husband's house, as I am of Hartfield' (p. 65). She admits that the first of these inducements should, as we have seen, be love, but mistakes her own potential for deep emotion: 'I never have been in love, it is not my way, or my nature; and I do not think I ever shall' (p. 65).

Wrong as she is on this score, her guess as to the other inducements is borne out by the fate of other women in the novel. In Miss Bates Jane Austen presents a touching picture of the spinster who lacks Emma's financial independence. It has often been remarked[12] that Austen, early in the novel, sets Miss Bates up as a foil to Emma in a descriptive paragraph which contrasts sharply with the opening description of Emma:

> Miss Bates was neither young, handsome, rich, nor married. Miss Bates stood in the very worst predicament in the world for having much of the public favour, and she had no intellectual superiority to make atonement to herself, or frighten those who might hate her, into outward respect. She had never boasted either beauty or cleverness.   (p. 14)

In at least one respect, however, Miss Bates and Emma are alike: Miss Bates's life is 'devoted to the care of a failing mother', as Emma's is to an ailing father (p. 14). Emma is no freer, in fact, than the spinsters and widows living in genteel poverty.

Miss Taylor, Harriet Smith, even the relatively wealthy Mrs Elton, *née* Augusta Hawkins, procure a house of their own, an establishment, through marriage. Only then do they attain relative independence. The only woman in the novel who appears to escape the general feminine plight of dependence and subordination is the great Mrs Churchill of Enscombe (whom we never actually meet). She does wield tremendous power, but we must recollect that she does so only by virtue of the accident of wealth, and of her conventional status as a married woman. Speculating at one point on the difference between Mrs Churchill's position in the world and Jane Fairfax's, Emma considers social injustice towards women: 'The contrast between Mrs Churchill's importance in the world, and Jane Fairfax's, struck her; one was every thing, the other nothing – and she sat musing on the difference of woman's destiny' (p. 301). But Emma's thoughts crystallise for us Jane Austen's sense that all the women in the novel are tied together by the common threat of 'woman's destiny', and that their destinies are more alike than different.

Mrs Elton unconsciously parodies the 'trade-unionism' of married women. She treats Emma, who is the same age, as a 'young lady on her preferment' (p. 277), and assumes that marital status automatically includes the right to dominate. Her attitude is an exaggerated result of the homage society pays to the married woman for her 'accomplishment'. One of her chief functions is to shatter comically Emma's illusion that even a wealthy single girl can have any meaningful precedence, prestige or liberty of movement. Jane Austen gives us a hilarious glimpse of Emma's dawning consciousness on the occasion of the ball: 'Emma must submit to stand second to Mrs Elton, though she had always considered the ball as peculiarly for her. It was almost enough to make her think of marrying' (p. 253).

Jane Fairfax is the principal foil to Emma in the novel: young, beautiful, clever and talented, but without Emma's added attribute of wealth. Jane is on the point of being sucked into the 'governess-trade' – for Jane Austen, as for Charlotte Brontë, a fate worse than death – when she is rescued by a timely marriage. Jane conceives of the profession as a quasi-religious sacrifice, to be met 'with the fortitude of a devoted noviciate' (p. 126).[13] When Mrs Elton urges her to seek a position immediately, Jane, though never a hysterical type, does not hesitate to equate 'governess-trade' with 'slave-trade': 'There are places in town, offices, where inquiry would soon produce something – Offices for the sale – not quite of human flesh – but of human intellect' (p. 233). Indeed, Jane leaves little doubt that she sees the position as a form of prostitution.

The four couples – Harriet and Robert Martin, Mr and Mrs Elton, Jane Fairfax and Frank Churchill, Emma and Mr Knightley – establish the social pattern of the novel. Starting at the lower end of the social scale with Harriet, Emma tries to match Harriet in turn with men of a higher and higher social class – Mr Elton, Frank – only to have her scheme ironically rebound on herself when Harriet begins to set her sights on Mr Knightley, the most incongruous jumping of class of all. There is poetic justice in the fact that it is Emma's own scheme which rebounds most seriously on her, not the Frank Churchill–Jane Fairfax scheme, which was largely Frank's creation. Emma is most snobbish about Robert Martin because she cannot play Lady Bountiful with the independent yeomanry:

The yeomanry are precisely the order of people with whom I feel I can have nothing to do. A degree or two lower, and a creditable appearance might interest me; I might hope to be useful to their families in some way or other. But a farmer can need none of my help, and is therefore in one sense as much above my notice as in every other he is below it.   (p. 20)

Mr Knightley, on the other hand – who is Jane Austen's spokesman on the subject of class structure – democratically substitutes the criterion of usefulness for inherited status. Accordingly, he values Robert Martin above the foppish Frank Churchill: 'His rank in society I would alter if I could. ... You laugh at me about William Larkins; but I could quite as ill spare Robert Martin' (p. 371). The yeomen may not own property, but they cultivate and enrich it, and may eventually become owners. As Trilling points out, 'the relatively easy recruitment to the class of gentlemen ... made England unique among European nations'.[14] Before we condemn Emma too readily for simple snobbishness, however, we must recognise that her feminism and her social conservatism are frequently in conflict. She is much like Dorothea Brooke who hopes for more misery in her clergyman husband's parish so that she can play an active role in alleviating it. Emma's usefulness, feminine usefulness, is contingent not on a knowledge of scientific farming, but on charitable volunteer work. She tries to assert an active feminine role within a relatively stable social order, without seeing that the latter will have to change as well to accommodate a more functional definition of woman's role.

THE FEMALE ARTIST: EMMA AND JANE AUSTEN

Implicitly, there is one creative outlet left for women, and that is Jane Austen's own – the artistic. At one point, as her social circle has begun to widen beyond Hartfield, Emma waits at the door of Ford's while Harriet frivolously examines the finery within. Emma looks out on her town, while we look in on her consciousness:

Much could not be hoped from the traffic of Highbury; – Mr Perry walking hastily by, Mr William Cox, letting himself in at the office door, Mr Cole's carriage horses returning from exercise, or a stray letter-boy on an obstinate mule, were the liveliest subjects she could presume to expect, and when her eyes fell only on the butcher with his tray, a tidy old woman travelling homewards from shop with her full basket, two curs quarrelling over a dirty bone, and a string of dawdling children round the baker's little bow-window eyeing the gingerbread, she knew she had no reason to complain, and was amused enough, quite enough still to stand at the door. A mind lively and at ease, can do with seeing nothing, and can see nothing that does not answer.

(pp. 179–80)[15]

As Lascelles notes, Emma's observation is trained on Jane Austen's own favourite subject matter, those 'pictures of domestic life in country villages' she had described to the Reverend Clarke in reply to his request that she undertake a historical romance. Jane Austen's own 'mind lively, and at ease' has no need of a 'subject', in the usual sense.

There is a marked disparity between this real material Emma is viewing, and her usual fantasies, nourished on romance and imagination. Jane Austen implies in this scene that the town could, should and perhaps will, in future, provide for her a lesson about the real material from which the artist must select.

As Emma's interest in Highbury increases, her efforts are diverted from explicit artistic acts – almost all of which occur in the first volume of the novel – to attempts at manipulating other people's lives. Her failings as an artist prefigure and epitomise her mistakes with life itself.

Mr Knightley, assessing Emma's course of reading, early provides us with the key to all of her deficiencies:

Emma has been meaning to read more ever since she was twelve years old. I have seen a great many lists of her drawing up at various times of books that she meant to read regularly through – and very good lists they were – very well chosen, and very neatly arranged – sometimes alphabetically, and sometimes by some other rule. ... But I have done with expecting any course of steady reading from Emma. She will never submit to any thing requiring industry and patience, and a subjection of the fancy to the understanding.   (p. 26)

Emma remains merely an 'artist figure' because the form she imparts to life is not original, nor does it arise naturally from the demands of the real materials. Using as characters her friends and

acquaintances, she attempts to combine elements from the old
romances she has read, instead of basing her work on acute
observation of life's own permutations and combinations. Emma is
guilty of a kind of authorial dabbling, of fanciful pastiche which
prevents her from creating a truly imaginative work with its own
impetus and inner logic.

Jane Austen summarises Emma's manifold half-accomplish-
ments, and thereby confirms Mr Knightley's judgement:

> Emma wished to go to work directly, and therefore produced the
> portfolio containing her various attempts at portraits, for not one
> of them had ever been finished, that they might decide together
> on the best size for Harriet. Her many beginnings were displayed.
> Miniatures, half-lengths, whole-lengths, pencil, crayon, and
> water-colours had all been tried in turn. She had always wanted
> to do everything, and had made more progress both in drawing
> and music than many might have done with so little labour as she
> would ever submit to. She played and sang – and drew in almost
> every style; but steadiness had always been wanting; and in
> nothing had she approached the degree of excellence which she
> would have been glad to command, and ought not to have failed
> of. She was not much deceived as to her own skill either as an
> artist or a musician, but she was not unwilling to have others
> deceived.   (p. 33)[16]

Apparently Emma has been trying to become the 'universal
artist', the Michelangelo or Leonardo da Vinci of Highbury, in
contrast to Jane Austen who could have said, along with Alfred de
Musset, 'Mon verre n'est pas grand, mais je bois dans mon verre.'
Emma has never been able to choose a single medium, never mind a
single style, in which to work, for she lacks all steadiness and
commitment.

Jane Austen may well be pointing with oblique irony, however, to
her own youthful failings in the 'juvenilia', spirited but relatively
uncontrolled, unpolished and formless parodies of romances. Most
important of all, however, this passage arouses our suspicions
about Emma's motives, doubtless unconscious, in turning to life
itself for her materials. She is (perhaps surprisingly) too good a critic
not to recognise her limitations as a genuine creative artist: there are
the half-finished sketches, the unplayable pieces, the unread books
before her to prove it. But with the intangibles of life, her delusions

can become monumental before the scales finally drop from her eyes. One suspects that she has taken as a challenge, instead of a reproof, Mr Knightley's sardonic comment on her so-called 'success' in matchmaking for Miss Taylor: 'Success presupposes endeavour.'

Not only does Emma take up the gauntlet and move into the sphere of action, but she interferes with people of whose lives she knows nothing but the social surface: Mr Elton, Harriet Smith, Frank Churchill, Jane Fairfax. Because she lacks knowledge of their deepest roots of personality, she treats them as if they were cardboard figures who had stepped out of one of her favourite romances. Although Jane Fairfax's situation would seem, at first glance, more romantic than Harriet's – we need only recall what Charlotte Brontë made of a similar situation in *Jane Eyre* – Jane Fairfax is not mere cardboard or malleable clay and resists all of Emma's efforts to probe her.[17]

With Harriet Smith, on the other hand, she can conjure up any imaginary past she chooses. Harriet is docile and pliable; all that is known of her is summarised in one short sentence: 'Harriet Smith was the natural daughter of somebody' (p. 15). Emma does not regard Harriet's illegitimacy as a stain provided that the girl is of noble birth, because in the romances heroes and heroines often turn out to be the lost or unacknowledged children of princes.[18] She imagines without compunction that Harriet's father's conduct is venial because he is noble; that Jane is having an affair with her best friend's husband, Mr Dixon; and even that Mr Churchill may have several natural children who would inherit his estate instead of Frank. Romances present only the glamorous side of such intrigues. As Mrs Lennox's Arabella is warned, a girl with any experience of the world would recognise that such 'adventures' probably never occurred at all, or if they did in the past, they could not now without casting grave aspersions on the moral fibre of the man or woman involved.

According to the morality of Emma's period, men should rise in the world only through ability, not through a marriage based on fortune-hunting. (In this respect Mr Elton violates Emma's code.) But it was considered not only permissible but desirable for a woman to rise, if she could, through marriage, as there was no other outlet available to her. In promoting Harriet's chances, Emma is not trying to revolutionise the social order; she remains somewhat of a snob. But she is leaning towards feminism in protesting the narrowmindedness of a society which refuses social betterment to illegitimate females who cannot make their fortune in 'masculine' ways.

When Mr Woodhouse says, 'Pray do not make any more matches', Emma fails to perceive the incongruities in her reply: 'I promise you to make none for myself, papa; but I must, indeed, for other people' (p. 6). She seeks, in other words, to exempt herself from the system in which she immerses Harriet, presumably because she sees herself triumphing through innate ability (like a man) instead of through a fortunate marriage.

Emma uses her concrete artistic endeavours to shore up and support her naïve *social* attempts at matchmaking. She begins with painting, moves to verbal art – criticising the style of Robert Martin's written proposal and modelling Harriet's letter of reply, inventing charades for the Riddle Book – and finally begins her most perilous 'game' of manipulating people in conversation in such a way as to imitate playacting.

The images of Mr Elton's charade reflect his greed for wealth, power and the secular life:

> My first displays the wealth and pomp of kings,
> Lords of the earth! their luxury and ease.
> Another view of man, my second brings,
> Behold him there, the monarch of the seas!   (p. 54)

If Emma were not so blinded and infatuated by her own schemes for Harriet, she could not miss the fact that Mr Elton has his eye on the 'luxury and ease' of the Woodhouses, and that Harriet could never be identified with the line, 'And woman, lovely woman, reigns alone', as the queenly and imperious Miss Woodhouse could.

With Emma's usual good taste, she perceives that all this is just inept if it applies to Harriet, but it never occurs to her that it might apply to herself: 'Thy ready wit the world will soon supply. Humph – Harriet's ready wit! All the better. A man must be very much in love indeed, to describe her so' (p. 55). Emma considers the charade to be a *verbal* portrait of Harriet, analogous to the oil portrait she herself has just painted. But in reality, both are portraits of Emma.

Emma is overly dependent on the reaction of her audience, almost willing herself to fall in love with Frank Churchill in order to satisfy the expectations of the Westons and other neighbours. She selects her materials arbitrarily, as when she fails to listen to Miss Bates reading Jane's letter in its entirety. Emma prevents us from

hearing and judging Jane Fairfax's epistolary style. She judges Jane
from her aunt's garrulity, and escapes the letters themselves
whenever possible. Had she listened, she might have learned
something not only about Jane's character, but also about her
proximity to Frank Churchill who was at Weymouth at the same
time.

Emma's verbal art, like her musicianship, reveals spirit, inven-
tion, and enjoyment, but inadequate technical control. As long as
her perceptions remained rooted in reality, however, Emma has a
certain deft articulateness. As Frank Churchill says, 'Miss Woodhouse, you have the gift of giving pictures in a few words' (p. 192).
She has, as well, a genuine gift for mimicry based on right
perceptions of the surface of manners and a keen sense of the
ridiculous. As an example, Lascelles cites the passage in which
Emma paints to Mrs Weston a satirical picture of Miss Bates's
hypothetical reaction were Mr Knightley to marry Jane Fairfax:

> How would he bear to have Miss Bates belonging to him? – To
> have her haunting the Abbey, and thanking him all day long for
> his great kindness in marrying Jane?
> – 'So very kind and obliging! – But he always had been such a very
> kind neighbor!' And then fly off, through half a sentence to her
> mother's old petticoat. 'Not that it was such a very old petticoat
> either – for still it would last a great while – and, indeed, she must
> thankfully say that their petticoats were all very strong.'
>
> (p. 174)[19]

Although Mrs Weston rebukes her, it is clear that she is also amused
by Emma's impressionistic ear which is so close to Austen's own:
'For shame, Emma! Do not mimic her. You divert me against my
conscience.'

A negative side of Emma's verbal art, however, is that she is
occasionally too prone to allow a sardonic and destructively critical
viewpoint to colour her statements. It is possible that Jane Austen,
once again, sees one of her own youthful weaknesses in this trait,
which, for Emma, reaches its *summum* of destructiveness in her
thoughtless cruelty to Miss Bates at Box Hill. There are witticisms
one can *think*, which are scarcely fit to utter.[20]

It is important to remember that Frank stage-manages this whole
episode. His directions for the game reveal his contempt for both
Highbury society and for Emma's perceptions. Having affronted

the audience by asserting Miss Woodhouse's already well-known desire to read the minds of all those present (as 'omniscient author'?), Frank adds insult to injury by implying that those present will find it easier to produce three dull thoughts than a single witticism. Much could be said in extenuation of Emma, who has suffered from the lack of wit and kindred spirits in Highbury, and of her need to impose some kind of aesthetic form on her milieu;[21] little can be said in justification of Emma's and Frank's callousness in criticising openly people of good will who, for all their intellectual inferiority, may nevertheless be aware of their own shortcomings and vulnerable to attack. Miss Bates, in fact, immediately exclaims, demonstrating her willingness to poke goodnatured fun at herself:

> 'Three things very dull indeed! That will just do for me, you know. I shall be sure to say three dull things as soon as ever I open my mouth, shan't I? ... Do not you all think I shall?'
>   Emma could not resist.
> 'Ah! ma'am, but there may be a difficulty. Pardon me – but you will be limited as to number – only three at once.'   (p. 290)

Emma's fault does not lie in her thinking that Miss Bates is 'prosy', but in her saying it in the hearing of this particular mixed company, many of whom already barely tolerate Miss Bates. Even Mrs Bates usually manages to turn a deaf ear to her daughter, but her hearing becomes remarkably better when Jane is staying with them.

Frank has set up the scene so that Emma will inevitably respond in just the way she does; even Miss Bates replies to Frank's suggestion with a joke at her own expense. Emma is tempted into a kind of playacting with Frank, so that she fails to see the dangers in such a dialogue when it is overheard in public. Emma is cruel not only to the aunt, but also to the niece, at Box Hill, but it is Frank who is consciously trying to hurt Jane by arousing her jealousy. He asks that Emma produce for him a wife 'like' herself, the opposite of Jane: 'She must be very lively, and have hazle eyes ... I shall go abroad for a couple of years – and when I return, I shall come to you for my wife. Remember?' (p. 292). But Emma is so wrapped up in her own 'play', composed around the central figure of Harriet, that she fails to see the purpose and intent of *Frank's*:

> Emma was in no danger of forgetting. It was a commission to touch every favourite feeling. Would not Harriet be the very

creature described? – Hazle eyes excepted, two years more might make her all that he wished. He might even have Harriet in his thoughts at the moment; who could say? Referring the education to her seemed to imply it.   (p. 292)

This substitution of Harriet for herself is very much the same mistake Emma makes with Mr Elton's charade and with her portrait of Harriet. She constantly refuses to assign herself the central role in the drama, preferring to be the playwright. Furthermore, she is not here consciously offending Jane, for she has never had the faintest glimmer of the relationship between Frank and Jane.

Portrait of Harriet

Emma's portrait of Harriet, which actually foreshadows all her other attempts at creativity, is a microcosm of Emma's talents and flaws. Modest about her own gift, Emma is perceptive about Mr Elton's lack of critical ability when he is assured of her skill at portraiture just because he has seen some of her landscapes: 'Yes, good man! – thought Emma – but what has all that to do with taking likenesses? You know nothing of drawing. Don't pretend to be in raptures about mine. Keep your raptures for Harriet's face' (p. 31). She is blind, however, to the fact that it is *her* face about which he is in raptures, making him negligent as to the quality of her drawing. She is oblivious to his real motives in watching every stroke of her painting. Ironically, she sees the whole situation as a play, but one in which she must be playwright and director, not heroine: 'he does sigh and languish and study for compliments rather more than I could endure as a principal' (p. 36).

Despite his obtuseness, his comment on the improvement of portrait over original reflects Emma's only half-conscious action: 'the attractions you have added are infinitely superior to what she received from nature' (p. 30). Emma has chosen Harriet as her subject because 'she thinks so little of her own beauty'. Ironically, it is Emma herself, and not Harriet, who is modest about her appearance. As Mr Knightley remarks, 'I love to look at her; and I will add this praise, that I do not think her personally vain ... her vanity lies another way' (p. 28). Her vanity is rooted in pride of intellect, not in physical attractiveness. Sometimes, however, her modes of expressing that pride clash; for instance, in her moment-ary vanity about her drawing, she forgets her primary motive of matchmaking. Seeing that Mr Elton is about to propose, as she thinks, to Harriet, she decides that, 'as she wanted to be drawing, the declaration must wait a little longer' (p. 33).

Jane Austen as omniscient author gives no direct description of the portrait; we perceive it only through the eyes of others. But it is easy to guess just whom Emma has really painted. In the chapter immediately preceding, Mrs Weston offers the only physical description of Emma in the novel: 'Such an eye! – the true hazle eye – and so brilliant! Regular features, open countenance, with a complexion? oh! what a bloom of full health, and such a pretty figure and size; such a firm and upright figure. There is health not merely in her bloom, but in her air, her head, her glance' (p. 28). We already have a description of Harriet: 'She was a very pretty girl, and her beauty happened to be of a sort which Emma particularly admired. She was short, plump, and fair, with a fine bloom, blue eyes, light hair, regular features, and a look of great sweetness' (p. 15).

The juxtaposition of these two descriptions suggests what Emma has done to the portrait. Mrs Weston, examining it, remarks, 'The expression of the eye is most correct, but Miss Smith has not those eye-brows and eye-lashes. It is the fault of her face that she has them not' (p. 35). The lashes and brows, presumably, are firm and dark, reflecting Emma's brunette colouring rather than Harriet's fairness. Mr Knightley remarks on the second fault of the painting: '"You have made her too tall, Emma"' said Mr Knightley. Emma knew that she had, but would not own it' (p. 35).

In question here is not Emma's artistic sense of proportion, but her intention: 'she meant to throw a little improvement to the figure, to give a little more height, and considerably more elegance' (p. 34). In other words, she made it resemble a tall, well-built but not plump, elegant young lady whose colouring (if not her hair) is brunette. The interplay of conscious and unconscious intention is most interesting: although Emma has chosen to improve Harriet's mien and figure, it is clear that she is unaware of drawing her criteria from her own appearance and bearing. This 'standing memorial of the beauty of one [Harriet], the skill of the other [Emma], and the friendship of both' is in reality a memorial to both the beauty and the skill of Emma Woodhouse.

For the most part, Emma resists playing the protagonist in her own 'romances'. Yet in the portrait episode she is both artist and, unconsciously, model. Her handling of the portrait might seem to support the hypothesis of such critics as Duffy and Mudrick – Emma can create a kind of Harriet–Emma figure in which Emma is the directing mind, Harriet a puppet merely responding to her cues.[22] Along with Mudrick, however, we cannot help asking, 'But why Harriet, of all people? and why so tenaciously Harriet, at least until every trick has failed?'[23] Agreed that Harriet is pliant, yielding and 'manageable', as Mudrick puts it; yet Emma could scarcely have found anyone so far removed from her own appearance and character merely to serve as an instrument of vicarious experience. Why cling to Harriet through all three volumes, as the girl becomes less and less manageable? And why does Emma 'particularly admire' this style of beauty so different from, and so obviously inferior to, her own?

Internal evidence points to the fact that Emma is completely lucid about Harriet's shortcomings. Far from being infatuated with her, as Mudrick supposes, she constantly points a finger of gentle scorn at her ignorance, incidentally contrasting it to her own wit. She knows full well that in painting Harriet, she has chosen a singularly inapposite proxy for herself.

Two chapters later, the explicit rhetoric of the novel yields the answer to the enigma. In the first Emma–Mr Knightley confrontation, the subject of the dialogue transcends Harriet's refusal of Robert Martin and expands to marriage in general and the situation of women. Bitterness underlies Emma's complaints about the masculine mastery of women: 'A man always imagines a woman to be ready for anybody who asks her' (p. 45).[24] She resents the fact that Harriet is, as Mr Knightley says, 'a girl who will marry somebody or other', a clinging, parasitical, fluffy-headed little blonde.

Emma uses Harriet as a support in her attack against the masculine judgement, which in her opinion loves appearance alone, whereas she sees her own character (ironically) as a triumph of brains over beauty: 'till it appears that men are much more philosophic on the subject of beauty than they are generally supposed; till they do fall in love with well-informed minds instead of handsome faces, a girl, with such loveliness as Harriet, has a certainty of being admired and sought after' (p. 47).[25]

She is scornful because men, according to her, not only reserve their highest admiration for that factor over which a woman has little control, personal beauty, but also actually prefer a mate who is silly and senseless, and therefore docile. Mr Knightley agrees that

Harriet is the nonentity her last name suggests, but for that very reason, he would not want her for a wife. In fact, he seems to prefer the challenge of Emma's intractable nature.

Emma despises both yielding women and the masculine judgement that supposedly sets them up for admiration. In Emma's most explicit diatribe against the narrowness and frivolity of the roles allotted to women by society, she adds a playful prediction that subsequently she unconsciously talks Harriet (and, almost, herself) into believing: 'I know that such a girl as Harriet is exactly what every man delights in – what at once bewitches his senses and satisfies his judgment. ... Were you, yourself, ever to marry, she is the very woman for you' (p. 48). Ultimately, Emma almost comes to believe that she has created in Harriet a kind of Frankenstein monster (before Mary Shelley's, of course). Mr Knightley, however, makes probably the most important statement in the novel about male–female relations: 'Men of sense, whatever you may chuse to say, do not want silly wives' (p. 48).[26]

Emma chooses Harriet as the overt subject for her portrait because she fits all the requirements for a heroine of romance – blonde, blue-eyed, passive, sweet, a fitting object for knight errantry.[27] But time and again, we learn that Emma does not really like the heroines of romances; she exhibits amused disdain for their failure to be active and vital like herself. There are in a sense two novels in *Emma*: Jane Austen's, in which Emma is the heroine, and Emma's, in which Harriet is the heroine. Emma recognises the spuriousness of the romances she has been reading, for she continually derides Harriet, the romantic heroine. Even when she praises Harriet's supposed 'tenderness', she assumes that it is incompatible with wit and concludes that she cannot emulate her friend: 'It was rather too late in the day to set about being simpleminded and ignorant' (p. 109).[28] Emma scorns a society which she believes values Harriet's attractions above her own. But she seems to have a perverse desire, against all evidence, to prove throughout the novel that she is right, that Harriet is, in fact, what men want. And what matter if logic fails in all this?

Emma's sister Isabella is doubtless a major contributing factor to Emma's thinking that even a man of sense prefers a silly wife. John Knightley, who falls little short of his elder brother in judgement – though far short in tact and breadth of interest – married Isabella, who has little to recommend her but tenderness and prettiness. Since Emma's love for Mr Knightley is present all along, but never consciously acknowledged, it is possible that some unconscious fear of his following his brother's example accounts in part for her vitriolic attack against the Harriets of this world, and against masculine judgement.

At one point Emma asks Mr Knightley, 'Does my vain spirit ever tell me I am wrong?' His reply is, 'Not your vain spirit, but your serious spirit. – If one leads you wrong, I am sure the other tells you of it' (p. 258).[29] Emma's deepest self knows that the real heroine of Emma's creation, and the real model for her portrait of Harriet, is Emma herself. It is Mr Knightley's difficult but joyous task to bring this 'deepest self' to the surface. By the end, he finds her 'faultless in spite of all her faults' – perhaps, I would add, faultless *because* of all her faults (p. 348).

Circles of Consciousness

Each of the characters in the novel possesses a certain circle of consciousness, of which the most restricted is Mr Woodhouse's valetudinarianism. While his criteria for judging people are all drawn from the world of health, they are not the less accurate for it. When, for instance, he decides that Frank Churchill is not quite the thing for leaving a door open and thus causing a draught, he is correct that this small act reveals Frank's general thoughtlessness and lack of consideration for others. At the other end of the scale Mr Knightley, the hero–teacher–critic, possesses the most all-embracing circle of consciousness in the novel. Jane Austen leaves little doubt that he will initiate Emma into *his* vision, as well as tying her own to reality.

Initially, Emma's perceptions, like her father's, are not inaccurate, but limited. For the poor, for example, she has considerable compassion and fellow-feeling:

> She understood their ways, could allow for their ignorance and their temptations, had no romantic expectations of extraordinary virtue from those, for whom education had done so little; entered into their troubles with ready sympathy, and always gave her assistance with as much intelligence as good-will.   (pp. 66–7)

Her perceptions are sharpened as her neighbourhood increases. With those characters about whom she cherishes no illusions, she can be fully realistic and even satirical. She recognises 'a sort of parade' in Mr Elton's speeches 'which was very apt to incline her to laugh': 'She ran away to indulge her inclination, leaving the tender and the sublime of pleasure to Harriet's share' (p. 63). Similarly, when she first meets Mrs Elton, she recognises her immediately for what she is: 'she suspected that there was no elegance; – ease, but not elegance. – She was almost sure that for a young woman, a stranger, a bride, there was too much ease' (p. 208). Emma has, in fact, predicted the Eltons' marriage, for she knows that her refusal of his proposal did not break his heart: 'He only wanted to aggrandise and enrich himself; and if Miss Woodhouse of Hartfield, the heiress of thirty thousand pounds, were not quite so easily obtained as he had fancied, he would soon try for Miss Somebody else with twenty, or with ten' (pp.104–5).

Emma's initial perceptions are usually accurate even with the complex characters. It is only when she tries to fit them into romantic preconceptions that she distorts the truth. It is not Emma's perceptions that are amiss, but her interpretations of them. She is perfectly correct, for instance, in guessing that Jane Fairfax's new pianoforte is an 'offering of love'; wrong in guessing that the 'lover' is Mr Dixon, whom she has never met, rather than Frank Churchill, whom she has, and about whom she is fashioning another romance altogether. Nor is she completely deluded by Frank's charm. Listening to him raving about Highbury as 'one's own country', Jane Austen gives us Emma's reaction: 'That he should never have been able to indulge so amiable a feeling before, passed suspiciously through Emma's brain' (p. 146).

Paradoxically, Emma's material mistakes and blunders grow steadily worse as her circle of consciousness widens and her perceptions sharpen. For twenty-one years Emma has been living a fanciful life. Box Hill is a last attempt to hold on to the fancy before she, like Don Quixote, 'explodes into sanity'.[30] This is her last desperate attempt to stop her ears against her 'serious spirit'. The result is comparable to a catharsis, a purgation: for the first time we see Emma wrenched with tears.

Her final step towards redemption occurs when she recognises the extent of her unconscious cruelty to both Harriet and Jane. She is unquestionably sincere when she perceives and empathises with Jane's anguish in figurative terms of torture, poison, battle: 'In Jane's eyes she had been a rival; and well might any thing she could offer of assistance or regard be repulsed. An airing in the Hartfield carriage would have been the rack, and arrow-root from the Hartfield storeroom must have been poison' (p. 316).

Only when she recognises the suffering of others does she perceive the strength of her own far-from-sisterly passion for Mr Knightley: 'It darted through her, with the speed of an arrow, that Mr Knightley must marry no one but herself!' (p. 320).[31] Since Jane Austen rarely uses figurative language in the Jamesian sense, the cluster of metaphors here reinforces the supposition that this period of awakened perception constitutes the turning point for Emma. From this moment on, she takes her place as heroine of the creation, not author or painter. Like 'Kitty, the fair but frozen maid' in the charade, she needs only to be awakened by some trouble which touches the deep springs of feeling in her.[32] At this point Emma's imagination no longer substitutes for an emotional life, but becomes an instrument of her emotions. The end of mental blindness comes with a flood of tears clearing the physical vision of illusions and enabling it to face reality: 'The blunders, the blindness of her own head and heart! – she sat still, she walked about, she tried her own room, she tried the shrubbery – . ... To understand, thoroughly understand her own heart, was the first endeavor' (p. 323). The irony here is that, as she admits, in 'one who sets up as I do for Understanding' of others, she has never taken the first step of understanding herself.

Not coldness, but self-projection, has been her flaw. She assumes that Frank Churchill has an open character because if she, Emma, were to speak as rashly and indiscreetly as he does, her motive would be openness and frankness. By the same token, Jane Fairfax must be emotionally cold because she is reserved: Emma herself could never be reserved unless she lacked feelings. She trusts that appearances reveal the whole depth of a personality to her keen perceptions.

Emma's Fate: the Incomplete Truth

In the final analysis, Emma possesses all of the qualities necessary for a heroine in a realistic romance, but only some of the qualities necessary to an artist capable of formulating an integral vision of life. Our curiosity about Emma's fate, however, remains somehow unsatisfied.[33] It is just as difficult to conceive of any diminution in the strength of her artistic drive as it is to imagine her ever

channelling it into an authentic work of art. At the end of the novel
she is already matchmaking for the tiny Ann Weston. A great deal of
the charm and fascination of the novel is due to the fact that its
heroine's ambitions and drives remain so much greater than the
outlets her society can afford, and so much greater than her own
articulateness and sense of form.

Following Mr Knightley's proposal to Emma and her acceptance –
'What did she say? – Just what she ought, of course. A lady always
does' (p. 338)[34] – Jane Austen, in one of her less subtle, and therefore
rare, editorial interventions in *Emma*, writes:

> Seldom, very seldom, does complete truth belong to any human
> disclosure; seldom can it happen that something is not a little
> disguised or a little mistaken; but where, as in this case, though the
> conduct is mistaken, the feelings are not, it may not be very
> material.   (p. 339)

Both the internal evidence of the text, and the general critical reaction
to it, would seem to suggest that this statement is at the heart of Jane
Austen's vision in *Emma*. As Emma recognises her limitations by the
end of the novel, Jane Austen seems herself to be aware that, at the
end, she is still leaving many questions unanswered.

All we can say of Emma's fate is that her imagination, corrected by
reality and Mr Knightley, finds its characteristic shape and form,
even though these may not correspond to her youthful dreams, or to
the artistic embodiment the reader might wish her to find. If Emma,
the would-be artist, has unconsciously painted a portrait of a realistic
heroine, herself, in altering her model, Harriet Smith, then Jane
Austen, the real-life artist, has by the same token succeeded in
painting a verbal self-portrait in Emma Woodhouse, the heroine
whose shortcomings she so narrowly escaped to achieve consumma-
tion in art, not life.

For those who wonder why Austen never produced a 'Portrait of
the Artist as a Young Woman', the answer is that she recognises she
herself is the exception, rather than the rule. She does come close in
this one novel, but prefers to offer us a heroine whose lot is the more
common one, even for gifted women – a heroine with whom we can
identify because we share her limitations.

Of all her novels, *Emma* is the one that comes so near to us that we
refuse to let go at the end. But, as Henry James was later to write
concerning the fate of Isabel Archer in his own 'Portrait of a Lady',

'The *whole* of anything is never told; you can only take what groups together'. The openness of the novel is not only that of life itself, but also that of the dynamic creative visions of Emma Woodhouse and Jane Austen.

3

Emma Bovary: Muse
in a
Shop Window

Why each is striving, from of old,
To love more deeply than he can?
Still would be true, yet still grows cold?
– Ask of the Powers that sport with man!

They yoked in him, for endless strife,
A heart of ice, a soul of fire;
And hurled him on the Field of Life,
An aimless unallayed Desire.

(Matthew Arnold, 'Destiny', 1852)

At first glance, the resemblance between Emma Woodhouse and Emma Bovary seems to end with their first name. In almost every nuance of character Flaubert's Emma is presented as the very antithesis of Austen's. Her complete destruction is inevitable from the moment of her first appearance in the novel.

Jane Austen's heroine is from the beginning simply 'Emma', as the title underlines, a forceful, dominant personality with a strong sense of identity. Flaubert's heroine, on the other hand, is identified principally as 'Madame Bovary', wife of Charles Bovary, doctor of Yonville. Few readers can recall without difficulty Emma's maiden name (Rouault), whereas they persist in thinking of the other heroines by their maiden names even after their marriages: Emma Woodhouse, Dorothea Brooke, Isabel Archer. As her identification only through marriage suggests, Emma Bovary is subjected to an even greater degree than the other heroines to the tyranny of her surroundings. Accordingly, Flaubert introduces us first to the schoolboy Charles Bovary, then to the various settings in which Emma's pathetic drama is to be enacted, before permitting us our first vision of Emma herself at Bertaux.

FROM HIGHBURY TO YONVILLE: THE ENGLISH PROVINCES AND THE FRENCH

In moving from the world of *Emma* to that of *Madame Bovary*, the reader receives the impression of leaving a soft, green English hillside for a dark, dank closet. Highbury is airy, invigorating, fresh; Yonville is claustrophobic. Emma Bovary frequently exclaims, 'J'étouffe! [I'm suffocating!]'. Surrey, Mrs Elton reminds us, is 'the garden of England'; despite her characteristic hyperbole, Austen validates this assertion in her own descriptions. Flaubert, on the other hand, describes the Norman countryside surrounding Yonville-l'Abbaye as a 'contrée bâtarde où le langage est sans accentuation, comme le paysage sans caractère [a bastard country where the language is without accentuation, as the landscape is without character]'.[1] Moreover, in contrast to the fertility of the Abbey Mill Farm, in this region 'la culture y est coûteuse, parce qu'il faut beaucoup de fumier pour engraisser ces terres friables pleines de sable et de cailloux [agriculture is costly here, because they need a great deal of manure to fertilise these powdery lands full of sand and stone]' (p. 66).

The French provinces are impervious to new social forces. They are absolutely stagnant; nowhere does one have a sense of the gradual, orderly changes affecting an amelioration of English provincial life. Despite all its melodrama, Emma Bovary's fate has absolutely no effect on the mediocre and static town: 'Depuis les événements que l'on va raconter, rien, en effet, n'a changé à Yonville [Since the events I am going to recount, nothing, in effect, has changed at Yonville]' (p. 68). Her corpse, at the end of the novel, seems to crumble into dust before our eyes and to float away into her surroundings, just as her character and aspirations have been overpowered by the town during her life: 'Emma disparaissait dessous; et il lui [Charles] semblait que, s'épandant au dehors d'elle-même, elle se perdait confusément dans l'entourage des choses, dans le silence, dans la nuit, dans le vent qui passait, dans les senteurs humides qui montaient [Emma was disappearing beneath it, and it seemed to him that, expanding beyond herself, she was getting lost confusedly in the surrounding of objects, in the silence, in the night, in the passing wind, in the moist smells which were climbing]' (p. 309). The meaninglessness of her fate is foreshadowed in the earlier scene in which Justin, Homais's apprentice, wistfully fondles her boots from which he is to clean the dirt and manure acquired during her morning walks to La Huchette to meet Rodolphe: 'il atteignait sur le chambranle les chaussures d'Emma, tout empâtées de crotte – la crotte des rendez-vous – qui se détachait en poudre sous ses doigts, et qu'il regardait monter doucement dans un rayon de soleil [he reached on the shelf for Emma's boots, all crusted with manure – the manure of rendez-vous – which crumbled into powder beneath his fingers, and which he watched climbing softly in a ray of sunshine]' (p. 176).[2] By the similarity of the two descriptions, Flaubert suggests the curious mix in Emma of romantic yearnings and earthiness, both of which are fated to return to dust, disappear, lose their identity in the amorphous atmosphere of Yonville. Both descriptions end with an upward movement signalled by the verb 'monter', but in neither case does this movement promise a fulfilment of Emma's aspirations; rather, it reveals ironically that they are cancelled out, nullified.

Yonville as Cemetery

Flaubert implies that the entire town is simply a large cemetery for all human hopes and ambitions. The gravedigger, Lestiboudois, is also the church beadle and the town handyman-gardener, profiting at the same time from the living and the dead. His gardening extends to the cemetery, where he grows potatoes, 'pommes de terre' (my emphasis), which are implicitly contrasted to the 'fruit d'or', the golden apple of happiness, sought by Madame Bovary. The curé admonishes him for his entrepreneurial activities: 'Vous vous nourrissez des morts, Lestiboudois! [You are nourishing yourself on the dead, Lestiboudois!]' (p. 68). This criticism expands to include the townspeople in general, who all feed on death. This early description of the town anticipates the later scenes in which Emma is first figuratively 'stripped' and laid out by her creditors, who evaluate her most intimate belongings, and then literally laid out at death, when even her supposedly faithful maid, Félicité, runs off with her finest dress.

The gravedigger's name suggests his function, as well as that of M. Homais, who battens on the sick, and of M. Lheureux, who battens on the poor. It contains a form of the two words, leste (quick) and boue (mud), implying that the outlook for victims of Yonville is to be buried quickly in the earth. At one point Flaubert writes of the cemetery as if it were tenanted by the living: 'toute cette portion nouvelle est presque inhabitée [all this new portion is almost uninhabited]' (p. 68). In the 'Comices agricoles' scene, Flaubert turns the tables and describes the living, gathering to hear the inane speeches, as though they were dead. Lestiboudois arranges the seats just as he arranges the tombstones, crowding them all together: 'Lestiboudois avait apporté là toutes celles qu'il avait déménagées de la prairie, et même il courait à chaque minute en chercher d'autres dans l'église, et causait un tel encombrement par son commerce, que l'on avait grand'peine à parvenir jusqu'au petit escalier de l'estrade [Lestiboudois had carried there all those he had moved from the field, and he even ran every minute to look for more in the church, and caused such a traffic jam by his business that it was very difficult for anyone to reach the stairway to the platform]' (p. 132). Even Emma Woodhouse's self-assertion would be restrained if she, like Emma Bovary, were afforded only the prospect of a 'living death'.

Yonville as Market

The town's character is expressed not only by the analogy to a cemetery, but also by Flaubert's frequent reminders that half the town's centre is nothing but a roofed-in market (p. 67). Diction relating to profit and loss used in connection with the cemetery reveals the close tie Flaubert establishes between the marketplace and death, or a living death. As in *Emma*, architecture reveals the essence of the tenant. The building that dominates the heart of Yonville is not the *mairie*, 'construite sur les dessins d'un architecte de Paris [constructed according to the plans of a Paris architect]', but the pharmacy of M. Homais, the product of eighteenth-century rationalism and materialism (p. 67). The step to nineteenth-century capitalistic exploitation was evidently easy for Homais. His door, with its gold letters on a black background, epitomises the coat of arms of the new 'aristocracy', the rising bourgeoisie. The colours are those of money or disease (yellow) and death (black). Flaubert thus places the responsibility for Emma's and Charles's deaths figuratively at Homais's door.

Emma is finally buried by the curé, Bournisien, and Homais, the 'little man' or 'homunculus', as he has been called, those two apparently antipathetic forces of the Church and of Science, the new god born in the eighteenth century. Bournisien himself, however, typifies the effects of the Enlightenment and Revolution on the

Church; from being merely corrupt in the eighteenth century, it has become totally ineffectual in the nineteenth.

Bournisien is as complete a materialist as Homais; when Emma appeals to him for spiritual strength, he, like Charles, sees her suffering only in terms of physiology. Because of the emphasis on mere physical well-being in these surroundings, Emma is in a sense as much the victim and prisoner as Emma Woodhouse of the closed private world of medicine, in this instance embodied by her husband and Homais. Science and materialism exclude humane concerns in favour of merely physical definitions of well-being. For Bournisien no one can be in agony but the ill and starving: 'j'ai connu là de pauvres mères de famille, des femmes vertueuses, je vous assure, de véritables saintes, qui manquaient même de pain [I knew there poor mothers of families, virtuous women, I assure you, real saints, who did not even have bread]' (p. 106). Ironically, it is the unsaintly Emma who reminds him that 'man does not live by bread alone': 'Mais celles, ... celles, monsieur le curé, qui ont du pain, et qui n'ont pas [But those women, ... those women, monsieur le curé, who have bread, and those who do not have]' (p. 106).

Various linked images of the novel remind us that bread, or material prosperity, is all that anyone ever offers to Emma. The last name of her great love, Rodolphe, is Boulanger, 'Baker', and he lives in La Huchette, which can be translated as 'the little bread box'. After Emma is abandoned by Rodolphe, her religious consolations are reduced to a sensual ecstasy experienced in taking the communion wafer representing the body of Christ: 'elle adressait au Seigneur les mêmes paroles de suavité qu'elle murmurait jadis à son amant, dans les épanchements de l'adultère [she addressed to the Lord the same suave words she had formerly murmured to her lover, in the ecstasies of adultery]' (p. 200). This sensuality never diminishes, for on her deathbed she kisses the body of Christ on the crucifix, evoking memories of the communion wafer (body of Christ) earlier: 'collant ses lèvres sur le corps de l'Homme–Dieu, elle y déposa de toute sa force expirante le plus grand baiser d'amour qu'elle eût jamais donné [gluing her lips to the body of the Man–God, with all her expiring force she bestowed on it the greatest kiss of love she had ever given]' (p. 301).

Not only does Emma herself confuse carnal and divine love, but others, perceiving her, experience similar confusion. When Charles first meets her at the farm at Bertaux, while she is still living in an innocent world of dreams, she is wearing blue, which, as Martin Turnell points out, is the characteristic colour for the Virgin's garments in medieval statues.[3] Soon after her marriage, Flaubert suggests her impending loss of innocence (adultery) by implicitly comparing her to the statue of the Virgin in the crumbling church at Yonville. Far from radiating purity and Christian faith, the statue, with its outlandishly rich and gaudy dress, resembles a pagan idol, 'vêtue d'une robe de satin, coiffée d'un voile de tulle semé d'étoiles d'argent, et tout empourprée aux pommettes, comme une idole des îles Sandwich [dressed in a satin gown, coiffed with a tulle veil studded with silver stars, with red painted cheeks, like an idol from the Sandwich islands]' (p. 67). We are forcibly reminded that the immediate cause of Emma's downfall is her vanity and extravagance in dress.

Emma is frequently seen in terms of the Cult of the Virgin. Rodolphe, Charles and Léon constantly refer to her as a madonna even when she is most, as Henry James puts it, rolling in the dust. When she is still resisting a potential liaison with Léon, she takes refuge in the 'Chapelle de la Vierge' in the Cathedral at Rouen. Flaubert later ironically underlines the failure of this refuge; after Léon has become her lover, one of her gifts to him is a medallion of the Virgin. Moreover, while her lovers are referring to her as angel, saint, madonna, Flaubert associates her with the fallen Eve. When she is striving with desperate intensity to hold on to Léon's fading love, Flaubert uses the image of a snake to describe her dress slipping to her feet (p. 262). He implies that she is an Eve who has already yielded to the blandishments of the serpent in the Garden – who is indeed almost in process of becoming the serpent.

Emma's Social Background

Albert Thibaudet remarks correctly, 'The world described in *Madame Bovary* is a world which is falling apart. ... But in every society when something is destroyed another thing takes its place.'[4] In post-Revolutionary France, there was no squirearchy or yeomanry, no Mr Knightleys or Robert Martins. There were only the bourgeoisie, the peasants and, in cities, the working class once the aristocracy had lost its power.

Père Rouault, Emma's father, is a peasant of the honest but unaspiring variety. Emma herself is socially beneath Charles, whose father is an ex-army doctor married to a hat merchant's daughter. Emma is the only one of our heroines who is a peasant in origin. Possibly because of her mother's ambition, she has received an education above her station, having been sent to a convent at the age of thirteen. Her 'belle éducation' contributed crucially to her downfall, for it encouraged her to fantasise a life based on her reading of Sir Walter Scott romances, Chateaubriand and Lamartine.[5] Nor do Emma's convent-acquired 'accomplishments' equip her for the only success open to anyone at this period, the accumulation of wealth: she had learned 'la danse, la géographie, le dessin, faire de la tapisserie et toucher du piano. Ce fut le comble! [dance, geography, drawing, tapestry work and piano playing. That was the limit!]' (p. 17). After Emma's death, her daughter Berthe descends beneath even her mother's peasant origins when she is forced to work in a factory.

THE ENCLOSED LIFE

The Heavens and the Pit

Georges Poulet asserts that Emma Bovary's life takes the form of a closed circle which grows narrower, pressing in upon her. Emma palpitates, attains an ecstatic state reinforced by her sensuality, strives to reach a mystical union with sky, moon, sun, sea, God, romantic love. Her dreams of freedom and escape take the shape of images of flight; but each attempt to take wing is accompanied by a gravitational pull towards the earthly prison. Jean Rousset gives a skilful interpretation of Flaubert's symbolic use of the high window from which Emma is constantly looking as permitting her ascendancy and a 'vue surplombante [downwards view]', shadowing forth her subsequent fall and its cause – the dichotomy between her inner, subjective, vision and the squalid reality of the town beneath her.

Not only does Emma dominate the scene from her window, but the villagers are also looking from their windows at Emma and pulling her earthwards with their spying and judgements on her conduct. At the beginning of the Yonville section, Emma accidentally meets Léon on the street and he accompanies her to her child's nurse: 'Dès le soir, cela fut connu dans Yonville, et Madame Tuvache, la femme du maire, déclara devant sa servante que

Madame Bovary se compromettait [By evening, this was known in Yonville, and Madame Tuvache, the mayor's wife, declared in front of her maid that Madame Bovary was compromising herself]' (p. 86). It is again Madame Tuvache – whose name means literally 'kills the cow', as 'Bovary' derives from 'boeuf' or 'bovine' – who witnesses Emma's real degradation at the end of the novel when she offers herself to M. Binet for money. As Stendhal wrote, 'Les moeurs sont pures en France dans les petites villes; chaque femme surveille sa voisine et Dieu sait qu'il n'y eut jamais de police mieux faite [Morals are very pure in little French towns; every woman spies on her neighbor, and God knows there was never a more able police force].'[6]

Emma identifies with birds soaring freely upward into the heavenly azure, with the 'hirondelle' or swallow. The only 'hirondelle' which appears in her life, however, is the coach of that name which conveys her to Rouen to her rendezvous with Léon. But that, we are never permitted to forget, is a return trip (as the swallow always returns to its point of origin). The 'Hirondelle', however, is far from birdlike; it is 'un coffre jaune porté par deux grandes roues qui ... empêchaient les voyageurs de voir la route et leur salissaient les epaules [a yellow box carried by two enormous wheels which ... kept the travellers from seeing the road and threw mud on their shoulders]' (p. 73). Rather than representing a path to the outside world, it is a completely closed-in box, almost a coffin, which does not even permit the traveller a perception of the roadside.

Again, listening to Lucie di Lammermoor's aria in the Rouen opera house, Emma too wishes to float freely into space like a bird: 'Lucie entama d'un air brave sa cavatine en sol majeur; elle se plaignait d'amour, elle demandait des ailes. Emma, de même, aurait voulu, fuyant la vie, s'envoler dans une étreinte [Lucie set out bravely on her cavatina in G major; she bemoaned her love, she was asking for wings. Emma, in the same way, would have liked to escape life, to take flight in an embrace]' (p. 208). But Emma never takes flight; her means of transport are the coach which muddies the travellers, and the horses which she and Rodolphe ride to their forest rendezvous. The horses also tramp through the mud, leaving their traces behind them (p. 151). Emma is at times reduced to trampling through the mud herself, or, worse than mud, 'la crotte des rendez-vous'. Finally she journeys through her society's sexual marketplace or barnyard at the end.

The recurrent motif of her muddy boots serves as ironic counterpoint to her desire for wings; it reminds the reader of her earthly, or earthy, ties, until we see Emma making her final descent into the earth: 'Elle descendait toujours' [She was still descending]' – all the way to hell, is perhaps the implication.

Emma is not the only character associated with the motif of the muddied foot. Charles first meets Emma when he goes to Bertaux, her father's farm, 'pour remettre un jambe cassée [to set a broken leg]'. Moreover, the little statue of the curé in her garden at Tostes loses its foot over the winter at the same time as Emma becomes totally disillusioned with her marriage.[7] This simple incident anticipates Emma's loss of virtue and religious faith, but also Hippolyte's loss of his foot when Emma inspires Charles to perform his great experiment with clubfeet. Hippolyte's operation, moreover, is linked descriptively and figuratively with Emma's terrible death scene. There escapes from his wound, as from Emma's mouth, 'un liquide noir [a black liquid]', symbol of her corruption, of all the lies she has told. Flies call attention horribly to Hippolyte's gangrenous leg, while Emma is surrounded by flies the very first time we meet her, in the kitchen at Bertaux: 'Des mouches, sur la table, montaient le long des verres qui avaient servi, bourdonnaient en se noyant au fond, dans le cidre resté [Flies, on the table, climbed along the glasses lying there, buzzed while drowning in the bottom, in the remaining cider]' (p. 21).[8]

The foot motif may also suggest that Emma is to learn both her 'idols', Rodolphe and Léon, have feet of clay. She addresses the unlikely Rodolphe in these terms: 'tu es mon roi, mon idole! tu es bon! tu es beau! tu es intelligent! tu es fort! [you are my king, my idol! you are good! you are handsome! you are intelligent! you are strong!]'. Only the last and perhaps the second quality attributed to him would be recognised by Rodolphe himself, however great his arrogance.[9] And finally, perhaps most obviously, the curé brings to mind Bournisien, whose religion is crippled, if not his physical being.

The sun and moon, also associated with flight or aspiration, function symbolically at significant moments in the novel. Emma, however, fails to recognise that there is a discrepancy between her romantically conceived notion of sun and moon, and her actual responses to them. She and Léon ecstasise over sunsets, each thinking they have found a kindred soul, an oasis in the desert of materialism. Actually, of course, their sentiments are banal and clichéd. Emma exclaims, 'Je ne trouve rien d'admirable comme les soleils couchants ... mais au bord de la mer, surtout [I find nothing so admirable as setting suns ... but beside the sea, especially]' (p. 76). Léon, with great originality, adds 'Oh! j'adore la mer [Oh! I adore the sea].'

Emma romanticises (as she learned to do in her convent days) to the point that she fails to see she is not telling the truth. In fact, it is frequently demonstrated throughout the novel that it is the sunrise she adores, and not the sunset. The sunset always makes her shudder, as if someone were walking over her grave. The futile interview with Bournisien takes place in the last rays of sunlight of the dying day: 'La lueur du soleil couchant, qui frappait en plein son visage, palissait le lasting de son soutane [The light of the setting sun, striking him full in the face, made his cassock seem pale]' (p. 104). Her final rejection by Rodolphe also takes place as 'la nuit tombait [night was falling]'.

Emma is in reality drawn towards the sensuous enjoyment of sunrise and daylight, but consciously attempts to subscribe to the conventional association of sunset or moonlight with romance. The moon glows while she and Rodolphe plot their elopement. On this perfect 'nuit d'amour' before the flight, Flaubert records the ironic counterpoint of their speeches, Rodolphe having already decided to abandon her:

– 'Ah! la belle nuit!' dit Rodolphe.
– 'Nous en aurons d'autres!' reprit Emma.

['Ah! what a beautiful night!' said Rodolphe.
'We will have others!' Emma replied.]   (p. 187)[10]

The moon is almost blood-coloured at this point, and makes the river beneath it resemble a snake, a motif already linked to Emma's role as Eve. Moonlight is mentioned one final time to describe Emma's wedding gown, now become her shroud: 'Des moires frissonnaient sur la robe de satin, blanche comme un clair de lune [Ripples shivered on her satin gown, white as a ray of moonlight]' (p. 309).

One final symbol related to the flight–freedom, earth–prison tension is that of the 'abîme' or pit which Emma frequently envisions opening beneath her feet. At the end symbol becomes fact as Emma is lowered into her grave. The one time she feels herself free is when, in the famous scene treated by Rousset, she is standing at the attic window after Rodolphe has abandoned her. She is 'free' to choose only one outlet in this milieu, and that is suicide, commitment to the abyss: 'Le rayon lumineux, qui montait d'en bas directement tirait vers l'abîme le poids de son corps [The luminous ray, climbing from below, drew the weight of her body directly to the abyss]' (p. 192). She can choose the oblivion of sunset, not the hope of dawn. She is, in fact, killing herself slowly throughout the novel, for her brain-fevers, or 'crises de nerfs', after each cataclysmic event in her life, are psychosomatic.[11] Poor Emma, married to a doctor when fifty years later she might have married a psychiatrist! It is also interesting to note that the last name of Emma's final lover, Léon Dupuis (Du-Puits; well or pit), suggests that he, along with Rodolphe, is responsible for casting Emma into the pit.

The Spatial Prison

Emma's life is circumscribed in the horizontal, or geographical, as well as in the vertical sense. Like Léon, she constantly complains of her fate, which is 'de vivre cloué aux mêmes endroits [to live nailed to the same places]' (p. 75). In fact, she blames the spatial confinement for the failure of her spiritual drives.

Compared to Emma Woodhouse, Emma Bovary has but a feeble, fragile imagination after all. From the moment we first see her, pricking her fingers sewing and sucking the blood, we realise that she is a sensualist whose imagination will require all the support it can muster from its surroundings: 'elle se piquait les doigts, qu'elle portait ensuite à sa bouche pour les sucer [she pricked her fingers, which she then brought to her mouth to suck the blood]' (p. 14). Another characteristic gesture is to bite her full lips, 'ses lèvres charnues [her full lips]' (p. 15). Similarly, for her imagination to encompass the splendours surrounding her at La Vaubyessard, she must call upon her sense of taste, as she 'fermait à demi les yeux, la cuiller entre les dents [she half closed her eyes, the spoon between her teeth]' (p. 49).

Emma marks the major divisions of her life by a series of movements in space. When she arrives at Yonville, she places all her hopes for a major future event on the prospect of further movement: 'Elle ne croyait pas que les choses pussent se représenter les mêmes à des places différentes, et, puisque la portion vécue avait été mauvaise, sans doute, ce qui restait à consommer serait meilleur [She did not believe that things could be the same in different places, and, since the portion she had lived had been bad, doubtless what remained to be lived would be better]' (p. 80).

Emma's entrapment both at Tostes and Yonville is frequently symbolised by the successive houses in which she lives. Domestic life, or household management, represents a prison for her: Père Rouault does not particularly miss her when she marries, for she has been of little use to him as a housekeeper. In this respect she is quite different from Emma Woodhouse, who takes pride in exercising a kind of domestic creativity. The house is literally a prison for her; Erich Auerbach discusses the resonances of the passage in which we learn that Emma is most aware of her boredom and entrapment at mealtimes: 'Mais c'était surtout aux heures des repas qu'elle n'en pouvait plus [But it was especially at meal hours that she could not endure any more]' (p. 61). This entrapment resembles that of Isabel Archer when she marries Gilbert Osmond; both Flaubert and James depict feelingly the horrors of sharing one's life with a person one despises. Flaubert vividly describes Emma's sense that 'toute l'amertume de l'existence lui semblait servie sur son assiette [all the bitterness of existence seemed served to her on her plate]' (p. 61).

It is during her stay in Tostes that Emma makes the first of her abortive attempts to escape the domestic or spatial prison. She and Charles are invited to a ball at La Vaubyessard by the marquis d'Andervilliers, whom Charles had treated for an abscess in his mouth. The marquis had been Secretary of State under the Restoration. Flaubert shows a certain ambivalence towards the aristocrats left over from the Louis-Phillippe era in this, one of the great scenes of the novel. The very ailment for which the marquis has been treated foreshadows Emma's death from arsenic poisoning. The Bovarys are invited because Emma seems more of a lady than a peasant. Characteristically, Charles virtually disappears during this episode. On their arrival, it is Charles's *carriage* we are aware of, not Charles himself, and the marquis greets only Emma. Emma later dismisses Charles for ruffling her gown (p. 47), and finally he is already sound asleep when she goes to bed to dream of the ball.

There are echoes of this scene throughout *Madame Bovary*. The organ grinder with his dancing monkey caricatures the ball. On the one hand, La Vaubyessard incarnates Emma's most cherished romantic reveries, which we have seen anticipated in her wedding cake, but demolished by the drunken orgies and revelry of her wedding day. And to a certain extent Flaubert reveals his roots in Romanticism by sharing Emma's dreams. On the other hand, he subtly undermines the decayed aristocrats who charm Emma. In fact, La Vaubyessard, and the place name may suggest *'veau'*, calf, tying it to the dominant animal imagery associated with both Emma and Charles.

The old men at the ball seem childish, the young men jaded, and both handle their women in the same manner as their horses, foreshadowing Rodolphe's treatment of Emma: 'à travers leurs manières douces, perçait cette brutalité particulière que communique la domination de choses à demi faciles, dans lesquelles la force s'exerce et où la vanité s'amuse, le maniement des chevaux de race et la société des femmes perdues [through their courteous manners penetrated that particular brutality communicated by the domination of half facile things, in which force is exerted and vanity amused, the handling of pedigreed horses and the society of fallen women]' (p. 48) The old roué, the marquis's father-in-law, who was reputed to have been Marie-Antoinette's lover, is an extreme example of this glamourised decadence which Flaubert mocks (p. 46). The horses in the stable are compared to kept women, and the petite Emma is herself implicitly likened to Charles's little horse, too small for its harness, pulling their carriage (p. 51). When Emma waltzes with the Vicomte – perhaps an echo of the seductive Vicomte de Valmont in Laclos's famous eighteenth-century epistolary novel *Les Liaisons dangereuses* – she becomes dizzy, like a horse out of control.

The reader receives an unreal, dreamlike impression at La Vaubyessard, as if its inhabitants were all moribund, as much relics of a long-dead past as their illustrious ancestors who appear in paintings on the walls. When correspondences with religion are played up, they are again moribund, ineffective, or trivial: the napkins are folded like a bishop's hat. Emma is overwhelmed by the world of material objects, as she will be at her death; fans, bouquets, flacons hide the features and individualism of the seated women. Emma herself is likened to an object, fixed and motionless: 'une statue de femme drapée jusqu'au menton regardait immobile la salle pleine de monde [a statue of a woman draped up to her chin, immobile, looked at the room full of people]' (p. 45).

The ball completes Emma's disenchantment with domestic life at Tostes. As Martin Turnell also points out, it creates an abyss in her life: 'Son voyage à La Vaubyessard avait fait un trou dans sa vie, à la manière de ces grandes crevasses qu'un orage, en une seule nuit, creuse quelquefois dans les montagnes [Her trip to La Vaubyessard had made a hole in her life, in the manner of those great crevices a storm, in a single night, carves sometimes in the mountains]' (pp. 52–3). She attempts to recreate her experience in memory, as she will later do with her love affairs, but the memory blurs as time lapses, if indeed it was ever sharp. Finally, she names her daughter Berthe after a young woman she had heard the marquis address by that name (p. 84); already disappointed she has had a daughter rather than a son, she has chosen a singularly inappropriate name for a daughter who will be downwards-mobile.

The futility and dissatisfaction Emma experiences in Tostes, apart from the brief respite at La Vaubyessard, are replicated in Yonville. When Emma first arrives in Yonville, palpitating with hope and desire, Flaubert describes the houses she passes: 'Les toits de chaume, comme des bonnets de fourrure rabattus sur des yeux, descendent jusqu'au tiers à peu pres des fenetres basses [The straw roofs, like fur hats pulled down over the eyes, descend almost to a third of the low windows]' (p. 66). These houses, personified as people with hats pulled deliberately over their eyes, resemble the Yonvillais Emma will soon meet, who blind themselves to anything outside their private worlds of finance, taxes and 'science'.

The image of entrapment, of house as prison, is intensified at Yonville. When Emma is standing at the attic window contemplating suicide, she is 'saved' not by the miraculous intervention of a romantic hero, or even of Charles suddenly become perceptive, sympathetic and understanding. She is merely recalled by Félicité to her prison, which she senses most vividly again at meal hours:

elle tressailit au contact d'une main sur sa manche c'était Félicité.
– Monsieur vous attend, Madame; la soupe est servie. Et il faillait descendre! il fallait se mettre à table!

[she shivered at the contact of a hand on her sleeve, it was Félicité.
– Monsieur is waiting for you, Madame, the soup is ready. And she had to go downstairs! she had to sit at the table!]   (p. 192).

At this point not only Emma, but also the reader, is forced to descend from a life-and-death crisis and watch Charles eating. And Charles displays his usual talent for doing the wrong thing at the wrong moment. The reader shares Emma's suffocation as Charles appeals to her ever-acute sense of smell, waving under her nose an apricot from the basket in which Rodolphe has sent Emma the note breaking off their projected elopement:

> – Sens donc! quelle odeur! fit-il en la lui passant sous le nez à plusiers reprises.
> – J'étouffe! s'ecria-t-elle en se levant d'un bond.
>
> [– Smell then! What a smell! he said in passing it under her nose several times.
> – I'm suffocating! she cried springing up suddenly.]   (p. 193)

Flaubert not only uses actual houses to suggest physical entrapment, as does Jane Austen, but also anticipates George Eliot and Henry James in the figurative use of architecture. At Tostes, for example, Emma foresees her future as 'un corridor tout noir, et qui avait au fond sa porte bien formée [a completely dark corridor, which had at the end of it a firmly closed door]' (p. 59). Again, after Léon leaves Yonville for Paris, her sorrow is equated with the wind whistling through an empty house: 'le chagrin s'engouffrait dans son âme avec des hurlements doux, comme fait le vent d'hiver dans les châteaux abandonnes [sorrow buried itself in her soul with soft moans, such as those made by winter wind in abandoned castles]' (p. 115). We are strongly reminded of George Eliot's description of Casaubon's mind as a bleak, dark, empty house, or of James's representation of Osmond's consciousness as a house in which Isabel Archer is incarcerated. The image serves a dual purpose: to reflect the heroine's physical confinement, and to reveal the spiritual poverty and emptiness which leave her no 'inner resources' after Léon's departure.

Whereas Emma Woodhouse found nourishment for her hungry imagination in a mere tableau of village life, Emma Bovary execrates it. She remains fatally convinced to the end that a change in locale would inevitably produce the romance she has been seeking.

There is no doubt that Flaubert intends to justify Emma's feeling of suffocation in the provinces, which he chooses as his background because he considers them the extreme embodiment of the evils of nineteenth-century French life in general. Because of the narrow confinement of the setting, the larger 'bêtise' and vulgarity of the age are magnified. If Highbury is a microcosm of all that is best in English life, Yonville is a microcosm of all that is worst in French life. It was undoubtedly to maintain the atmosphere of total confinement that Flaubert omitted from the final draft of the novel Emma's projected trip to Paris.

Similarly to Emma Woodhouse at the beginning of her educational process, Emma Bovary associates the unknown world outside the provinces with bodies of water. Paris resembles a vast ocean, and Emma's dreams of escape are connected with the sea. As she plans to run away with Rodolphe, 'au galop de quatre chevaux [to the gallop of four horses]', she dreams of living in a cottage 'au bord de la mer [beside the sea]', and of being cradled by the water in a Venetian gondola (p. 183).[12]

Granted the unprepossessing nature of her society, and her own inability to come to terms with it, it is no wonder that her fate is to move only from one cell to another of her spatial prison. Two closely related incidents vividly reveal the tension between opposites in Emma's own character, which keeps her forever locked within the prisonhouse of self, as well as within the provincial prison.

At the very beginning of the marriage she throws kisses and flowers to Charles from the window. Confined within the house, she leans out of the window, yearning to make her marriage correspond to the passions she has encountered in books. Flaubert emphasises her sensuality, the very antithesis of a romantic, vaporous imagination: she tears the flowers with her mouth, and her peignoir falls open. She never learns to weave into a coherent whole the two seemingly warring elements of her personality, romanticism and voluptuousness:

Elle se mettait à la fenêtre pour le voir partir; et elle restait accoudée sur le bord, entre deux pots de geraniums, vêtue de son peignoir, qui était lâche autour d'elle ... elle continuait à lui parler d'en haut, tout en arrachant avec sa bouche quelque bribe de fleur ou de verdure qu'elle soufflait vers lui et qui, voltigeant, se soulevant, faisant dans l'air des demi-cercles comme un oiseau, allait, avant de tomber, s'accrocher aux crins mal peignés de la vieille jument blanche.

[She stood at the window to watch him leave; and she remained with her elbows on the sill, between two pots of geraniums,

dressed in her peignoir, which hung loose around her ... she
continued to speak to him from above, while tearing with her
mouth a bit of flower or leaf that she blew towards him and which,
flying, lifting, making semicircles in the air like a bird, would,
before falling, become tangled in the unkempt mane of the old
white mare.]   (pp. 31–2)

This rich passage employs the simile of a bird to describe the flowers
she throws, again suggesting her wish to take flight. But the flowers
do not even reach Charles, for they become entangled with the
horse's mane, suggesting the animalism both within and without
Emma. Multiple references to animals – not only in this scene but
also in the description of Père Rouault's farm, in the 'Comices
agricoles' scene, in Charles's last name, in the analogy between
Rodolphe's horsemanship and mastery of women – permit us to
interpret the setting of the novel as just one enormous barnyard.

A second scene illuminating Emma's plight is that in which we
see her at the window of the completely enclosed coach, returning
from her rendezvous with Léon, throwing kisses at her lover, who
presumably has already returned home and is not there to receive
them. She sobs wildly to fan the flames of her passion: 'Emma se
mettait à genoux sur les coussins, et elle égarait ses yeux dans cet
éblouissement. Elle sanglotait, appelait Léon, et lui envoyait ses
paroles tendres, et des baisers qui se perdaient au vent [She was on
her knees on the cushions, and her eyes rolled in the dazzling light.
She sobbed, called Léon, and sent him tender words, and kisses
which were lost on the wind]' (p. 248).

This last love of Emma's is a complete artifice, an artistic creation
analogous to that Emma Woodhouse instigates with Frank
Churchill, who has much of Léon's foppishness and dilettantism.
Emma seems to have expended the last of her natural self in the
liaison with Rodolphe, so that we can say of her love for Léon, 'Elle
se bat les flancs pour sentir [She whipped herself into feeling].'
She writes a long series of imprudent love letters to Léon, not to
express her true feelings, but because heroines of novels always
give epistolary vent to their passions: 'Elle n'en continuait pas
moins à lui écrire des lettres amoureuses, en vertu de cette idée,
qu'une femme doit toujours écrire à son amant [She continued
nevertheless to write him love letters, by virtue of the idea, that a
woman must always write to her lover]' (p. 270).

Presumably, the kisses she throws from the coach to Léon, like those she throws from the house to Charles, do not attain the lover, but melt into the surroundings, as she does herself at the end of the novel. The only response to them emanates from the blind beggar who follows the coach. The blind man becomes a powerful symbol, an externalisation of all Emma's own failings. Flaubert at this point tells us something of the little song which he sings, an ironic commentary on Emma's situation:

> Souvent la chaleur d'un beau jour
> Fait rêver fillette à l'amour

Et il y avait dans tout le reste des oiseaux, du soleil et du feuillage.

> [Often the heat of a beautiful day
> makes a young girl dream of love

And there was in all the rest birds, sunshine and foliage.]

(p. 248)

All these motifs are closely connected with Emma herself, but the birds, leaves and other conventions of romantic poetry are not really the elements which create love in the poem; they are merely ornamental. In fact, love is caused by heat, by a warmth in nature that operates on man in the same manner as it does on animals. Beneath the surface romanticism of the blind man's song, as beneath Emma's life, there pulsates a simple eroticism, a sensuality pushed beyond the bounds of reason.

Flaubert originally intended to make the beggar armless and legless instead of blind; this detail would obviously have reinforced the symbolism attached to earthiness, to crawling through mud and eventually returning to dust. But in the final version this symbolism yields to a more important Flaubertian stress on the theme of perception. The beggar is not only blind, but eyeless, because Flaubert wants to comment on Emma's own lack of perception; she too is completely closed in, deluded, unable to escape the prisons of her own body and mind, through which there continually echoes a romantic refrain similar to that croaked by the beggar. Her eyes are weapons to strike a lover, or shields from a curious husband, but never instruments of perception. Were the scales ever to drop from her eyes, however, there would be no hope of compromise between actual and ideal, as there is for Emma Woodhouse.

At Emma's death the chorus figure of the 'aveugle' appears mysteriously in Yonville, once again outside her window. This time we hear the entire song, which has a galvanic effect on Emma, and serves as her death blow:

> Souvent la chaleur d'un beau jour
> Fait rêver fillette à l'amour.
> Pour amasser diligemment
> Les épis que la faux moissonne,
> Ma Nanette va s'inclinant
> Vers le sillon qui nous les donne.
> Il souffla bien fort ce jour-là,
> Et le jupon court s'envola!
>
> [Often the heat of a beautiful day
> Makes a young girl dream of love.
> To gather diligently
> The grain the scythe cuts
> My Nanette bends
> Towards the furrow yielding it.
> It blew very hard that day,
> And the short skirt blew away!]   (pp. 302–3)

The erotic planting and harvesting symbolism takes on a new dimension juxtaposed to Emma's final agonies, for the 'sillon' for which she is headed is the grave, her final spatial prison, rather than a symbol of fertility. The song also serves to remind us of Emma's peasant origins and of the animal imagery pervading the book. The wind blowing the short skirt evokes Emma stripped naked by her creditors. Our final impression is of an existence that has carried so little weight on the earth, had so little impact, that when it is whirled away by the wind, it is as though Emma had never lived in the first place: 'Elle n'existait plus [She was no longer existing]' (p. 305).

We learn later that the blind man is in Yonville because he has been inveigled by M. Homais into trying a miraculous cure for his loathsome skin disease. Although Homais is never directly responsible for anything that happens to Emma, Flaubert implies his indirect responsibility for her death since, first of all, it is his poison she takes, and secondly, the blind man who so terrifies her is there at Homais's behest. The blind man is also identified with Emma by their joint victimisation at the hands of the pharmacist. When the latter fails to cure him, his presence in town becomes a living reproach to Homais, who finally succeeds in having him committed to an asylum.

Harry Levin mentions that the song is by Restif de la Bretonne, which further calls into question its apparent romanticism.[13] Flaubert, first of all, juxtaposes Emma's romantic palpitations and the horrors of the old man's appearance. Secondly, he underlines the grotesqueness of a song about dreams of love which issues from the lips of a degraded specimen of suffering humanity. In addition, it is curious that Flaubert has chosen verses, not by one of his loved-and-despised romantic poets, but by the eighteenth-century novelist Restif, whose works were licentious, scabrous. The song itself, which can be read as a piece of disillusioned cynicism, encapsulates the novel's basic tension between romantic illusion and materialism.

The Prison of Womanhood

If Emma's entrapment is caused by her material and spiritual poverty, it takes the particular form it does because she is a woman. As Paul De Man points out, Emma is literally a prisoner of her marriage because she can move about spatially only within the limits of the one region in which Charles is licensed to practise medicine.

Emma Woodhouse believes that, for a woman of independent means, marriage is not a necessary step in the educational process. She can explore for herself what are usually considered the 'masculine' provinces of knowledge. The kind of knowledge Emma Bovary wishes to gain, however, can only be taught her by a man, on whom society imposes fewer moral restrictions and obligations. Emma dreams of the ideal hero–teacher – whom Jane Austen's heroine finds in Mr Knightley – but what Emma Bovary wants to be taught are new passions, sensations, movement, activity, not fine moral or aesthetic discrimination: 'Un homme ... ne devait-il pas tout connaitre, exceller en des activités multiples, vous initier aux mystères de la passion, aux raffinements de la vie, à tous les mystéres? [A man ... should he not know everything, excel in multiple activities, initiate you in the mysteries of passion, the refinements of life, all the mysteries?]' (p. 39).

Her imprisonment with each of the three men in her life is figured by some physical image of enclosure. The physical entrapment with Charles has its objective correlative in the walls of the house, penetrated only by the window. The window is merely a narcissistic reflection of Emma, however, and does not permit her a perception of external reality. Her loss of independence with Charles is suggested when his love congeals into a mere habit on the same level as their meals: 'Ses [Charles's] expansions étaient devenues régulières; il l'embrassait a de certaines heures. C'était une habitude parmi les autres, et comme un dessert prévu d'advance, après la monotonie du diner (His overtures had become regular; he embraced her at certain hours. It was a habit among others, and like a dessert foreseen in advance, after the monotony of the dinner]' (p. 41).

The liaison with Rodolphe begins promisingly in the forest and continues with Emma's morning walks to La Huchette. But soon the physical dimensions contract, constricting her even more than the marriage. Her relationship with Charles has at least the entire house as its setting; that with Rodolphe moves prudentially from a natural setting to the tunnel in her own garden, and finally to Charles's consulting room. The tunnel is particularly revealing as an image of enclosure; when Rodolphe meets her there, he had 'un grand manteau; il l'en enveloppait tout entière [a great cloak; he covered her entirely with it]' (p. 157). He takes complete possession of her; so she no longer exercises free will, and we feel that this self-abnegation is what she has sought all along, contrary to her protestations.

The setting is not appropriately romantic, for the season is all wrong. Flaubert, demonstrating that the love is 'out of season', pricks holes in the romantic notion that nature reflects and sympathises with man's feelings. Like Stephen Crane, he would say that nature is 'indifferent, flatly indifferent'. As the physical restrictions imposed on their love by the weather worsen, their affair becomes increasingly like a marriage, so that 'quand le printemps arriva, ils se trouvaient, l'un vis-a-vis de l'autre, comme deux mariés qui entretiennent tranquillement une flamme domestique [by the time spring came, they resembled a married couple quietly maintaining a domestic flame]' (p. 159).

Although Emma proclaims her desire for freedom, she paradoxically demonstrates a desire to be possessed completely by a man. The needs of her woman's nature are often contradictory. In the relationship with Rodolphe, Emma even comes to rejoice in her chains, crying to her lover: 'Il y en a de plus belles; mais, moi, je sais mieux aimer! Je suis ta servante et ta concubine! (There are more beautiful women; but I, I know better how to love! I am your servant and your concubine!]' (p. 178). It is not Emma, but Rodolphe, who finally tires of this 'amour-habitude': 'Emma ressemblait à toutes les maîtresses; et le charme de la nouveauté ... laissait voir à nu l'éternelle monotonie de la passion, qui a toujours les mêmes formes et le même langage [habitual love: Emma resembled all mistresses; and the charm of novelty ... exposed the eternal monotony of passion, which always has the same forms and the same language]' (p. 178).

With Léon her life constricts again before our eyes. The irregular, excessive, almost unnatural character of this relationship is symbolised by Flaubert's description of the coach in which it all begins. The coach offers a perfect image of enclosure, windows shut and blinds drawn. It is compared to both a boat and a tomb, reinforcing the association of unregulated passion with death (p. 228). Both coach and horses are treated anthropomorphically. The coach 'vagabonda' ['wanders'], as Emma herself does both here and at the end of the novel. The exhaustion of horses and coachman, 'presque pleurant de soif, de fatigue et de tristesse [almost weeping from thirst, fatigue and sorrow]' (p. 228), the animal heat, foreshadows her end when she is almost driven to walk the streets begging for money. It is as though the passion were itself driving the coach, shutting it off from the rest of the world. That this passion blinds them, rather than widening their vision, is underscored by the fact that the coach literally runs through scenes depicting the entire history of Rouen, both ecclesiastical and political, for Flaubert mentions every major monument and park they pass. But they see nothing of all this, for the blinds are drawn. Emma must always shut off the real world in order to enjoy the dream, thus blinding herself.

In a strange variation on her first adultery, Emma attempts a role reversal with Léon, playing the masculine role and teaching him the art of love. Jane Austen's Emma shared with men only a drive for intellectual power. Emma Bovary imitates them in dress, wearing a 'gilet' or man's waistcoat doubtless inspired by 'dandysme', as Baudelaire recognises, or smoking one of Rodolphe's cigars.[14] Even when she does not herself try to assume masculine prerogatives, she asserts that only men are free, and the best she can hope is to live vicariously through a son (p. 83).

Emma is at her lowest point when she attempts to corrupt Léon, as Rodolphe had previously corrupted her: 'il devenait sa maîtresse plotôt qu'elle n'était la sienne. ... Où donc avait-elle appris cette corruption, presque immatérielle à force d'être profonde et dissimulée [he becomes her mistress more than she his. ... Where then had she learned this corruption, almost immaterial by virtue of being profound and disguised]' (p. 201). Rodolphe has been her teacher, in a far different sense from Mr Knightley with Emma Woodhouse: 'Il jugea toute pudeur incommode. Il la traita sans façon. 'Il en fit quelque chose de souple et de corrompue [He judged all modesty useless. He treated her callously. He made of her something supple and corrupt]' (p. 179). Emma tries to avenge herself on all men by assuming a masculine role with Léon. In her vehemence, she exclaims, 'Vous êtes tous des infames! [You are all infamous!]', incidentally revealing to Léon that he is not her first affair.

Despite her attempt to master Léon, Emma remains the slave. Once again the affair becomes a habit, and once again it is the man who tires first of the monotony. His letters become a compendium of romantic clichés: 'il était question de fleurs, de vers, de la lune et des étoiles, ressources naïves d'une passion affaiblie, qui essayait de s'aviver à tous les secours extérieurs [it was a question of flowers, poetry, of the moon and stars, naïve resources of a weakened passion, trying to fan its flame by external aids]' (p. 262).

All three imprisonments with men lead only to her final enclosure within not one coffin, but three: 'quand les trois couvercles furent rabotés, cloués, soudés, on l'exposa devant la porte [when the three covers were planed, nailed, soldered, it was exposed in front of the door]' (p. 310). The effect conveyed by the triadic verb forms, corresponding to the three coffins, is that of Emma now nailed down and imprisoned forever. It is as though Emma herself were exposed in the street to public ridicule. The novel also comes full circle at the end. Emma's story begins when she becomes 'Madame Bovary' and ends with her return to Charles to die. Ironically, she does succeed in imposing her own vision and dreams on a man, Charles, but after her death and without even trying to: 'Elle le corrompait par delà le tombeau [She was corrupting him from beyond the grave].'

EMMA WOODHOUSE AND EMMA BOVARY:
FANCIFUL IMAGINIST AND SENTIMENTAL IMAGINIST

Unrepentant to the end of the affair, when she is disappointed with

Léon, Emma experiences again the tenacious dream of the ideal hero–teacher:

> en écrivant, elle percevait un autre homme, un fantôme fait de ses plus ardents souvenirs, de ses lectures les plus belles, de ses convoitises les plus fortes.

> [while writing, she saw another man, a phantom composed of her most ardent memories, her most beautiful readings, her strongest desires.]   (p. 270)

This passage illuminates some of Emma's fundamental failings as an artist figure. We can sympathise in part with her failure, given the tawdriness of the milieu, but we must also admit that her imagination is itself tawdry. Flaubert indicates that she lacks a vivid imagination unless it is stimulated by the senses. Conjuring up an ideal lover, she 'en palpitait émerveillée, sans pouvoir néanmoins le nettement imaginer, tant il se perdait comme un dieu, sous l'abondance de ses attributs [palpitated in a daze, without nevertheless being able to imagine him clearly, so lost he was like a god, beneath the abundance of his attributes]' (p. 270). Such a lover would inhabit a dream world: 'la contrée bleauâtre où les échelles de soie se balancent à des balcons, sous le souffle des fleurs, dans la clarté de la lune [the blueish country where silken ladders hang from balconies, beneath the scent of flowers, in the clear moonlight]' [p. 270).

However limited her potential, however great her need of external stimulus, Emma remains none the less an 'imaginist' of sufficient power to experience sensually all the raptures of physical love by just dreaming about it: 'ces élans d'amour vague la fatiguaient plus que de grandes débauches [these waves of vague love fatigued her more than great debauches]' (p. 270). At the end of her life, she prefers dream to reality, wishing even that she had never left the convent.[15] Of her girlhood, Emma thinks, 'Quel calme dans ce temps-là! Comme elle enviait des ineffables sentiments d'amour qu'elle tâchait, d'après les livres, de se figurer [What calm in that time! How she envied ineffable love sentiments that she tried to imagine, according to books]' (p. 263). So vivid is her imagination that, when she is finally rejected by Rodolphe, as she finds her desperate way home, she recreates in memory their entire love story. She pushes totally from her consciousness her very real financial straits, the immediate cause of her last appeal to Rodolphe, and abandons herself totally to reverie: 'elle ne se rappelait point la cause de son horrible état, c'est-à-dire la question d'argent. Elle ne souffrait que de son amour [she had no memory of the cause of her horrible state, that is the question of money. She suffered only from her love]' (p. 291).

In a sense, *Emma* and *Madame Bovary* are the closest in intention and theme of the four provincial novels. Both Emmas are 'imaginists'; the differences lie in what stimulates their imaginations. Both Austen and Flaubert are inspired by the *Don Quixote* tradition, more directly than either Eliot or James, and by the desire to puncture unrealistic romance. Austen was writing realistic fiction shortly after the heyday of the Gothic tradition, and contemporaneous with the Scott romance. Flaubert is writing in retrospect, when realism has already taken the lead from romanticism. As Thorlby has suggested, *Don Quixote* 'is misled by his imagination, Emma by her feelings'. She is a 'Female Quixote' who becomes a victim of Romanticism, as Alain-Fournier has called her.[16] Jane Austen's Emma, on the other hand, blends the romantic and the idealistic, much like the Don himself. As Charlotte Ramsey Lennox and Austen both knew, Cervantes's Don had his Dulcinea del Toboso as well as his windmill. Emma Woodhouse sees herself as a knight-errant in matchmaking.

'The Novel within a Novel': Emma's Artistry

As in *Emma*, there are really two concurrent novels in *Madame Bovary*, two creators. The 'novel', or perhaps we should call it a 'romance', created by Emma Bovary, is sentimental and abortive; the novel of Gustave Flaubert is realistic, disenchanted and a successful distillation of its heroine's foolishly sentimental Quixotism. Flaubert chooses a woman as his 'creative' figure because the remorseless logic of the book requires a protagonist who is powerless to escape the provincial milieu, even by subjective means. If Emma's consciousness is, as Henry James proclaims, 'really too small an affair', Flaubert himself is only too aware of it. Art requires two qualities, Flaubert wrote to Louise Colet, 'faith and freedom'.[17] Emma possesses neither. Freedom, he said, requires 'keeping all my other passions locked up in cages'.[18] The Romantics do not keep their 'passions locked up in cages'; rather, like Emma, they exploit them, or project themselves narcissistically.

Emma Bovary's girlhood introduction, in the convent, to music, art and literature, like Emma Woodhouse's, affords some clues as to why she develops the artistic temperament, but one which is badly flawed. An entire chapter is devoted to the literary aspect of her socialisation. Books teach her to reduce nature to a double of her self, 'etant de tempérament plus sentimentale qu'artiste, cherchant des émotions et non des paysages [being of a temperament more sentimental than artistic, seeking emotions and not landscapes]' (p. 34). Her eye is never on the object; rather, it is absorbed into her inward vision: 'Elle n'aimait la mer qu'à cause de ses tempêtes, et la verdure seulement lorsqu'elle etait clairsemée parmi les ruines [She loved the sea only for its storms, and grass only when it was studded among ruins]' (p. 34). She demands that reality objectify her dreams, or else the latter will die of inanition. We have seen the very real houses she inhabits, but she is convinced that the 'history' romanticised by fiction is actual fact; that, had she only been born in another time or another place, life would correspond to her dreams. Even on her deathbed, she never abandons the conviction that life is romantic, and that it is merely her ironic fate to have been imprisoned in one of the few prosaic corners of the universe.

Emma exercises editorial selection analogous to that practised by Jane Austen's Emma. When she reads history, she focuses on the role of women and attaches greater importance to the king's mistresses than to the king himself.[19] Both Emmas evince characteristically feminist presentiments. What many critics have called Emma Bovary's 'masculinity' seems, in fact, to be an extreme outgrowth of her feminist sense of frustration at having to live in a 'man's world'.

The true artist, in contrast to Emma, who remains locked in inner vision, projects his inward vision outward until it becomes absorbed by the object and he loses all sense of personal identity. Thus when Flaubert composes one of the love scenes, he tells Louise Colet in a letter, 'I am in the midst of lovemaking; I am sweating and my throat is tight.'[20] It is in this sense that he becomes Madame Bovary. Describing the forest seduction, he writes, 'Today, for instance, man and woman, lover and beloved, I rode in a forest on an autumn afternoon under the yellow leaves, and I was also the horse, the leaves, the wind, the words my people spoke ... even the red sun that made them shut their love-drowned eyes. ... Is it a silly overflow of exaggerated self-satisfaction, or is it really a vague and noble religious instinct?'[21] Flaubert's worship of form does, indeed, become for him a kind of secularised religion. He once said that he was a mystic at heart, and believed in nothing. In point of fact, he believed in the Palace of Art.

Another flaw in Emma's artistry is her confusion of sentiment with sentience (or her tactile sense). She has chosen the wrong artistic models: *Paul et Virginie*, Bernardin de Saint Pierre's exotic tale of youthful platonic love, Chateaubriand's *Génie de christianisme*, Sir Walter Scott's historical romances, Lamartine's poetry – all of them romantic works expressing vague, vaporous yearnings, whose heroes are models of purity, virtue and fidelity: 'messieurs braves comme des lions, doux comme des agneaux, vertueux comme on ne l'est pas, toujours bien mis, et qui pleurent comme des urnes [gentlemen brave as lions, gentle as lambs, virtuous as no one is, always well dressed, and weeping like fountains]' (pp. 34–5).

She loves sermons because, with their 'comparaisons de fiancé, d'époux, d'amant céleste et de mariage éternel [comparisons of fiancé, husband, celestial lover and eternal marriage]', she confuses mystical ecstasies with sensual (pp. 33–4). As a girl she loves the touch, the feel of her romances, their 'belles reliures de satin (beautiful satin bindings)' (p. 35), as much as the romances themselves.

But undoubtedly Emma's major fault as an artist is her inarticulateness, her lack of awareness of the exigencies of form, which might have objectified and corrected her sentimentality. Flaubert implies, however, that the failure is not entirely Emma's own. She has been raised in a society that cares little for the truth of words, but only for platitudes. She has learned the use of language from literature which, from Flaubert's point of view, relies on vague emotionalism rather than on exactitude and an ordered, reasoned view of life. From Emma's experience, Flaubert generalises about the failure of language in our everyday dealings; everything we say becomes either a mere formula or a tissue of lies. When Emma utters platitudes to Rodolphe about her very real passion, Flaubert comments bitterly, 'la parole humaine est comme un chaudron fêlé où nous battons des mélodies à faire danser les ours, quand on voudrait attendrir les étoiles [human speech is like a cracked cauldron where we beat melodies to make bears dance, when we want to make the stars tender]' (p. 179).

All of Emma's artistic failings, which we perceive early in our convent training – self-projection, confusion of sentimentality with sentience, of mystical with sensual ecstasy, the mistaking of fiction for reality, the lack of articulateness – manifest themselves with much more serious consequences in her later life.

When she cries, 'j'ai tout lu [I have read everything]', after her introduction to marriage, it is because she seeks to turn from books to life. She wants to play a central role in a drama, not – like Emma Woodhouse – to create a new artistic work herself. Her art is not disinterested in Flaubert's terms. She does not scruple to use her interest in music as a pretext to further her intrigue with Léon. She is enraptured with the opera only until Léon appears: 'Mais à partir de ce moment, elle n'écouta plus [But from that very moment, she ceased to listen]' (p. 212). Flaubert compares her to Legardy, the tenor in the opera, who has 'plus de tempérament que d'intelligence et plus d'emphase que de lyrisme [more temperament than intelligence and more emphasis than lyricism]' (p. 208). Flaubert, on the other hand, views the depersonalisation of the artist as a strength and a duty.

When Emma recalls the beginning of her relationship with Rodolphe, she prefers the poetic recreation in memory to the act itself. To that extent she is a genuine artist who requires the solitude of her dream world. She rids herself of Charles in order to dream of Rodolphe in the isolation of her bedroom:

> Et, des qu'elle fut débarrassée de Charles, elle monta s'enfermer dans sa chambre. D'abord, ce fut comme un étourdissement; elle voyait les arbres, les chemins, les fossés, Rodolphe, et elle sentait encore l'étreinte de ses bras; tandis que le feuillage frémissait et que les joncs sifflaient.
>
> Mais, en s'apercevant dans la glace, elle s'étonna de son visage. Jamais ell n'avait eu les yeux si noirs, ni d'une telle profondeur. Quelque chose de subtil épandu sur sa personne la transfigurait.
>
> Elle se répétait: 'J'ai un amant! un amant!' se délectant à cette idée comme à celle d'une autre puberté qui lui serait survenue.[22]

[And, as soon as she got rid of Charles, she went upstairs to shut herself in her room. At first, it was like a dizzy spell; she saw

trees, roads, ditches, Rodolphe, and she still felt the embrace of
his arms; while the foliage shivered and the reeds whistled.

But, seeing herself in the mirror, she was astonished at her face.
Never had her eyes been so black, nor so deep. Something subtle
permeating her person was transfiguring her.

She repeated to herself: 'I have a lover! a lover!' delighting in
this idea as in that of another puberty happening to her.]

(pp. 151–2)

Emma is an artist, but a self-centred one. Her selfishness is most
evident in her treatment of the child Berthe, whom she even injures
physically, albeit inadvertently (p. 108). Flaubert imputes her
callousness in part to her peasant upbringing, which keeps
'toujours à l'âme quelque chose de la callosité des mains
paternelles [always in the spirit something of the callousness of the
paternal hands]' (p. 62). A 'fanciful imaginist' like Emma
Woodhouse, on the other hand, would plan enthusiastically for her
little girl's future. Emma discounts Berthe because she is not a son,
and because she resembles her father (Berthe is blonde). She is
therefore a constant reminder of the tepid banality of her existence
with Charles.

Not only Emma's mother love, but also her religious faith,
subserve the tyranny of selfhood. The 'trinity' of men in her life
corresponds in some ways to the Father, Rodolphe, who dominates
and teaches her; the Son, Léon, whom she in turn dominates and
teaches; and the Holy Ghost, Charles, who finally participates in her
dreams and continues in a sense the strivings of her soul. Emma
expropriates the ritual and mythology of her religion to satisfy her
own sensual needs. Even her philanthropy is motivated by
Rodolphe's abandonment and leads to excess and temporary
madness.[23] We are reminded in one scene of the debauch in the
film *Viridiana*, in which the devout heroine takes tramps and
beggars into the house, only to have them take command and
overrun it. Similarly, Emma 'se livra à des charités excessives. ...
Charles, un jour, en rentrant, trouva dans la cuisine trois vauriens
attablés qui mangeaient un potage [gave herself up to excessive
charities. ... Charles, returning one day, found in the kitchen three
tramps sitting at the table eating soup]' (p. 201).

Emma's sexual development also exhibits disorder and confusion. First, she experiences marriage without love with Charles; next,

physical love and sexual initiation with Rodolphe; and finally, sentimental or romantic love with Léon.

Portrait of Emma: Miniature or Muse?

Unlike Emma Woodhouse, Emma Bovary herself makes no attempt to embody her ideals concretely in art. But like Austen's heroine, her character and ultimate fate are revealed by association with certain works of art, the miniature, for instance, which Charles has had painted of her. Of our four heroines, only Emma's character is represented by a miniature rather than a large oil canvas. She is a physically small woman, not very healthy or robust, who must wear dark clothes to add elegance to her figure. Her 'walks' are not a product of a youthful health and high spirits, as are Emma Woodhouse's, or Dorothea Brooke's and Isabel Archer's; they are, rather, devoted to adultery.

Emma's fate and that of the miniature are closely paralleled. Caring little that the portrait was a gift from her husband, she presents it to her lover; he tosses it carelessly in a box, among trifles from other mistresses already cast off. He notices only the artificial pose and unfashionable taste of the portrait, not its subject's genuine passion: 'sa toilette lui parut prétentieuse et son regarde en coulisse du plus pitoyable effet [her attire seemed pretentious to him and her sidelong regard a pitiful effect]' (p. 187). When he rummages through the box, he breaks locks of hair given him as favours, which probably anticipates the death scene when Homais cuts a souvenir lock from Emma's head, pricking her temples.

But Emma is also the picture of a muse which her second lover, Léon, has seen in a shop window.

> Il y a sur le boulevard, chez le marchand d'estampes, une gravure italienne qui représente une Muse. Elle est drapée d'une tunique et elle regarde la lune. ... Quelque chose incessamment me poussait là.

> [There is on the boulevard, in the engraver's shop, an Italian etching representing a muse. She is draped in a tunic and looking at the moon. ... Something incessantly pushes me there.]   (p. 217)

Flaubert implies that if Emma herself cannot create art, she could at least have served as Muse or inspiration for a true poet. But Léon is no poet. Or, as Flaubert comments, 'Le plus médiocre libertin a rêvé des sultanes; chaque notaire porte en soi les débris d'un poète [The most mediocre libertine has dreamed of sultans; each little notary carries within him the débris of a poet]' (p. 269). The authentic poet is outside the novel; the poet inspired by this Muse is Flaubert himself. Unlike Léon and his probable master Alfred de Musset, he recognises a woman like Emma for what she is; like Baudelaire, he affirms that art can find beauty even in the mud. This Muse, moreover, is found in a shop window, offered for sale, as Emma herself is finally in spite of her protest: 'Je suis à plaindre, et non à vendre [I am to be pitied, not to be sold]' (p. 287). Instead of inspiring art, at the end of the novel Emma is degraded and sent forth into the marketplace by a crass and commonplace society.

Art in the Marketplace

Despite all of Emma's failings, she retains our sympathy for her blind 'strivings' towards an 'aimless unallayed Desire' which she cannot even define. She loses all desire for Léon, for example, when she finds 'dans l'adultère toutes les platitudes de mariage [in adultery all the platitudes of marriage]' (p. 269). In a milieu given over to animalism and avarice, she at least retains an ideal of love, and cares nothing for money. She is never even conscious of it save to procure the luxuries which feed her imagination. She is negligent, fails to see how the money is instrumental to the adultery, when for the rest of her society money is the only driving force.

In the 'Comices agricoles' scene, we receive a vivid impression of the philistinism of this society. The comments of Lieuvain, the principal speaker, about agriculture serve as ironic commentary on Rodolphe's pseudoromantic language which veils his animalism. Lieuvain (lieu commun?) pays only lip service to 'art' or 'intellig-ence', for the key to this society is a narrow utilitarianism:

> où trouver, en effet, plus de patriotisme que dans les campagnes, plus de dévouement à la cause publique, plus d'intelligence en un mot? Et je n'entends pas, messieurs, cette intelligence superficielle, vain ornement des esprits oisifs, mais

plus de cette intelligence profonde et modérée qui s'applique pardessus toute chose à poursuivre des buts utiles, contribuant ainsi au bien de chacun, a l'amélioration commune et au soutien des Etats, fruit du respect des lois et de la pratique des devoirs.

[where can we find, in effect, more patriotism than in the countryside, more devotion to the public cause, in a word, more intelligence? And I do not mean by that, gentlemen, that superficial intelligence, the vain ornament of lazy spirits, but rather that profound and moderate intelligence which is applied above all else to the pursuit of useful ends, thus contributing to the good of all, to the common improvement and sustenance of the States, the fruit of the respect for law and the practice of duty.]   (pp. 134–5)

No wonder Flaubert can find no refuge in life itself! The import of this speech is that, contrary to what Lieuvain thinks he is saying, post-Revolutionary France leaves no hope for dreams of glory. Art, which could give order to this confused babble, is pushed well into the background as the 'vain ornement des esprits oisifs'.

Francis Steegmuller reports that Flaubert had deeply divided feelings about the Emperor Napoleon III. On the one hand, he admired success, and came to see himself as a 'furious aristocrat' (like those of La Vaubyessard?). On the other hand, he saw no hope in politics – nor indeed in life itself. He remarked that "89 destroyed royalty and the nobility, '48 the bourgeoisie, and '51 the people. There is nothing left but a bestial and imbecile rabble, and the only way to live in peace is to place yourself above the whole of humanity to be a simple spectator.'[24] Only this 'simple spectator' was above all an artist, and the final refuge is the Palace of Art: 'Equality is slavery. That is why I love art: there, at least, all is liberty in a world of fictions.'[25]

Yonville's idea of artistry is best exemplified by M. Homais. He is a journalist who rounds off the rough edges of truth and reports Emma's death as an accident, not a suicide, thereby depriving it of the last vestige of dignity. He finally writes a book and begins to affect 'le genre artiste [the artistic temperament]'. This book, a statistical survey of the provinces, reveals only cold facts, unlike Flaubert's 'Moeurs de province':

il etouffait dans les limites étroites du journalisme, et bientôt il lui fallut le livre, l'ouvrage! Alors il composa une *Statistique Générale*

du canton d'Yonville, suivie d'observations climatologiques, et la
statistique le poussa vers la philosophie. Il se préoccupa des
grandes questions: problème social, moralisation des classes
pauvres, pisciculture, caoutchouc, chemins de fer, etc.

[he stifled in the narrow confines of journalism, and soon he
needed to produce the book, the work! Then he composed a
*General Statistics of the Canton of Yonville, Followed by Climatological
Observations*, and statistics urged him towards philosophy. He
was preoccupied with great questions: social problems, the
morality of the poor, fishing, rubber, railroads, etc.]   (p. 319)

Emma's romantic dreams seem noble by comparison to Rodolphe's
callousness, Léon's calculating escapism, and Homais's journalism.[26] Flaubert shares with his heroine, though on a far more
conscious and articulate level, the rejection of the values of the
marketplace.

Flaubert once commented bitterly to George Sand about his age:
'The whole dream of democracy is to elevate the proletariat to the
level of stupidity of the bourgeoisie.'[27] Especially in a provincial
setting, the creative mind encounters formidable obstacles to
change. Flaubert, like Matthew Arnold, felt what it is like to be
'Wandering between two worlds, one dead, / The other powerless
to be born.'[28] As Baudelaire recognised, the most effective way to
'épater le bourgeois [to crush the bourgeoisie]' (when he reads
fiction) is to place him in a provincial setting, whose narrowness and
pettiness reflect the narrowness and pettiness of his own mind.
Analysing Flaubert's novel, Baudelaire so penetrates his mind that
he adopts his voice in attempting to reproduce the *genèse de l'oeuvre*:

since of late our ears have been assaulted by infantile chatter of
a group of theory-makers and since we have heard of a certain
literary device called *realism* – a degrading insult flung in the face
of all analytical writers, a vague and overflexible term applied by
indiscriminate minds to the minute description of detail rather
than to a new method of literary creation – we shall take
advantage of the general ignorance and confusion. We shall apply
a nervous, picturesque, subtle and precise style to a banal canvas.
We shall make the most trivial of plots express the most ebullient
and ardent feelings. Solemn and definitive words will be uttered
by the silliest of voices.

'And where can we find the breeding-ground of stupidity, the setting that produces inane absurdities and is inhabited by the most intolerant imbeciles?

'In the provinces.

'What characters, in the provinces, are particularly insufferable?

'Petty people in petty positions, with minds distorted by their actions.

'What is the tritest theme of all, worn out by repetition, being played over and over again like a tired barrel-organ?

'Adultery'.[29]

Flaubert, in a letter of appreciation for Baudelaire's article, wrote, 'You have penetrated the inner mystery of the work as if you and I shared the same mind. You have felt and understood me entirely.'[30]

'MADAME BOVARY, C'EST MOI'

When Flaubert says, 'Madame Bovary, c'est moi', he is referring to a special kind of identification with his heroine, which permits him sometimes to become part of her, and sometimes to stand aside dispassionately and judge her. His narrative technique sometimes induces us to share her rhapsodies. It is possible to forgive her for feeling revolted when Charles 'lui donnait sur les joues de gros baisers à pleine bouche [gave her on her cheeks fat, wet kisses] (p. 32). At other times, as during the death scene, our sympathies are anaesthetised, and we even share the scientific curiosity attributed to Flaubert in the famous caricature in which we see him dissecting Emma Bovary. Both objective and empathetic views are balanced when Rodolphe seduces Emma: 'elle sentait son coeur, dont les battements recommençaient et le sang circuler dans sa chair comme un fleuve de lait. ... Rodolphe, le cigare aux dents, raccommodait avec son canif une des deux brides cassée [she felt her heart, which began beating again while the blood circulated in her body like a river of milk. ...: Rodolphe, with a cigar between his teeth, fixed with his knife one of the two reins which was broken]' (p. 150). Rodolphe's indifference underlines Emma's love of an unworthy object. Flaubert suggests animalism on both sides by the simile he uses to describe Emma floating on a sea of assuaged passion. It resembles not simply a river, but 'un fleuve de lait [a river of milk]', returning us to the barnyard level. In effect, he is calling Emma a cow, an analogy reinforced by her married name and invoked when she goes to La Huchette by crossing 'le plancher aux vaches [the cow bridge]'.

The artist is not consistently throughout in the position of the caricatured Flaubert plunging a scalpel into Emma's heart. This movement in and out of Emma's consciousness provokes a certain malaise on the reader's part. Although at times Flaubert subjects Emma to ruthless analysis, his sympathies (and ours) constantly waver and vacillate.

The creator's partial identification with his creation helps explain the diversity of critical reactions to *Madame Bovary*. As with Austen's *Emma*, the critics' response depends to a great degree on their partisanship or antipathy towards the heroine. Reactions to her range between the two extremes of Matthew Arnold and Baudelaire. Comparing the novel to *Anna Karenina*, Arnold writes:

> But *Madame Bovary*, with this taint, is a work of *petrified feeling*; over it hangs an atmosphere of bitterness, irony, impotence; not a personage in the book to rejoice or console us; the springs of freshness and feeling are not there to create such personages. Emma Bovary follows a course in some respects like that of Anna, but where, in Emma Bovary, is Anna's charm?[31]

Baudelaire, on the other hand, rhapsodises over Emma's poetic, if misguided, power: 'she gives herself with magnificent generosity, in an entirely masculine manner, to fools who don't begin to measure up to her, exactly as poets will put themselves at the mercy of foolish women'.[32]

When we discuss Flaubert's attitude, we are inclined to speak of his points of view in the plural. The irony and the sympathy operate simultaneously much less consistently than in Austen's *Emma*. When he is involved with his Emma, he is much more so than Jane Austen is with hers; when he is ironic, he is much more cruelly ironic than she. The two do not seem to me, however, to blend into a perfect whole. Flaubert's provincial heroine wavers before our eyes; when we speak of Emma Bovary, we often seem to have taken the Emma of one particular scene for the whole woman. And, as different readers seize on different scenes, she remains a curiously unresolved figure, woven of disparate threads.

Flaubert could not, as consistently as Austen, make the point of view the heroine's own because her mind *is* rather too small an affair. Were we to remain wholly locked within Emma's consciousness, the result might be rather close to Molly Bloom's soliloquy, but without Molly's saving graces of humour and awareness. Emma Bovary is completely lacking in the wit and capacity for self-criticism that constitute in good measure Emma Woodhouse's charm.

Although Flaubert sympathises entirely with Emma's desire to revolt against the surrounding mediocrity, he cannot condone the manner of her revolt. It is not Emma's fault that her imagination has been conditioned by romanticism, the dominant aesthetic of a time when the majority culture had no interest whatsoever in aesthetics. Romanticism is infinitely preferable to the materialistic philosophy of M. Homais, to the materialistic business of M. Lheureux, and the materialistic religion of the curé Bournisien. In the last analysis, Flaubert's own temperament is fundamentally more romantic than realistic: 'I am at home in the realm of the extraordinary and the fantastic, in flights of metaphysics and mythology.'[33] It has long been noted that Emma is a 'feminisation' of Flaubert's own romantic nature, frequently subject to dreams and hallucinations.

When Flaubert was at the height of his creative powers, the prevailing literary mode was Realism, itself a reaction against Romanticism. Although he is most often defined as a realist, speaking of *Madame Bovary* he writes, 'it was in hatred of realism that I undertook this book'.[34] Life is an illusion, a phenomenon viewed subjectively by different individuals. If Philistinism has triumphed over Romanticism, it is only fitting that Flaubert should use the literary 'device' of Realism, so dear to the bourgeois heart – as in M. Homais's ultimate exercise in realism, uninterpreted statistics – to paint the death throes of the earlier school. His sympathies in the death struggle, however, are clearly less with the killer than with the slain. Realism becomes for Flaubert a middle-class weapon turned against the middle class. He uses it to paint a portrait of the forces rejecting or negating his art. Reality is Yonville, life driven into the narrowest and most provincial of corners. Romanticism is unwilling to cope with reality; Realism accepts it without offering any alternatives or possibilities of change. *Madame Bovary* has often been taken to be a book about the failure and death of Romanticism, incarnated by Emma, but it is equally a book about the failure of Realism.

The Palace of Art

Flaubert is more formalist than realist. His minute realistic details are informed by an overall *architectonike*. And if the public will not read him, then the public be damned! Threatened with extensive cuts and censorship of *Madame Bovary*, he prefers not to publish than to accept alteration.

Aesthetic form constitutes the only cathedral in which the artist worships. To achieve structural perfection is an agonising process for a man whose instincts tend to the romantic and sensual. At times Flaubert resembles the Gide of *Les Faux-Monnayeurs*, who determines 'not to take advantage of the momentum of the work'. Flaubert's ideal, expressed to Louise Colet, was to write 'un livre sur rien [a book about nothing]', a book which 'would be held together by the strength of its style'.[35]

Madame Bovary approaches this ideal. He deliberately chose as subjects a society and a heroine presenting no possibility of external or internal order. The *donnée* of the work is that the 'Palace of Art' must exclude not only a mediocre bourgeoisie, but also all would-be artists like Emma who are incapable of self-discipline. Mary Lascelles tells us that Austen wrote *Emma* easily in a particularly happy and productive one-year period; Flaubert took four and a half years to write *Madame Bovary*, reading children's books, keepsakes and much-hated romances in order to document his work meticulously. At one point he complains, 'I am doing no more than five or six pages a week.'[36]

Austen, Eliot, even James would have found Flaubert's Palace of Art lofty and admirable, but also claustrophobic. Their three heroines comparable to Emma appear in *Bildungsromans*; through suffering they arrive at awareness. *Madame Bovary* is a *Bildungsroman* turned upside down; it is about a woman incapable of growth, and it is the forerunner of the twentieth-century anti-novel.

Flaubert himself may have found his Palace of Art suffocating. In terms of formal perfection, *Madame Bovary* is the most integrated of our four novels. In terms of psychological realism, however, the novel seems evasive, indistinct, slips through our fingers. His theory of art demands the complete rout of Emma's aspirations. He grants to Emma much of his own poetic temperament: the ability to recreate an act in memory, the preference for recreation over the act itself, tactile sensitivity. Flaubert was inclined to make life subserve art; critics suspect, for instance, that he resumed his affair with

Louise Colet in order to gather material on the feminine response to love and sexuality.[37]

Flaubert does not, however, grant Emma his own ability to objectify and transform. As Emma Woodhouse may have been Jane Austen's sardonic portrait of herself at an early age, so Emma Bovary may well be Flaubert's portrait of himself as he was in his youth, fascinated by a humourless, unjudging Romanticism. It is of the essence in the portrait that Emma, who, unlike Flaubert, clings tenaciously to her romantic vision, be totally defeated. Emma remains to the end 'repliée sur elle-même [inwards-turning]' in the Romantic sense, as Flaubert is not. She is not, therefore, finally an artist.

Despite the inevitability of Emma's total destruction, demanded by Flaubert's rigorous theory, something in her dies hard. He *thinks* that only those who take refuge in art can successfully resist provincial mediocrity. But something fiercely tenacious in Emma's imagination lives on in Charles even after Flaubert has disposed of her as cruelly and as definitively as possible.

The Charles of the early scenes is very like Emma in his simple sensuality, and the Charles of the end almost *becomes* Emma, laying her out for burial in her bridal gown, a gesture worthy of Emma herself, and beginning to perfume himself. In his original version of the novel, Flaubert was tempted to relieve the bleakness of the work and provide a triumph of perception for Charles, and by extension for Emma herself. De Man underlines the importance of this draft passage which contrasts Rodolphe's lack of empathy with Charles's selfless love for Emma:

> For he [Rodolphe] understood nothing of that voracious love which throws itself upon things at random to assuage its hunger, that passion empty of pride, without human respect of conscience, plunging entire into the being that is loved, taking possession of his sentiments, palpitating with them and almost reaching the proportions of a pure idea through generosity and impersonality.[38]

But Flaubert's logic compelled him to excise this poignant, moving passage from the final version. To have included it would imply that Emma succeeded at least once as an 'artist' by making Charles share her vision. And that success cannot be permitted if such transcendence comes only to the authentic, producing artist.

There is something summary and unconvincing about Flaubert's build-up of Charles only to kill him off too.

As Benjamin F. Bart remarks, Flaubert recognised that his views on art could have little relevance to those of us who are not artists: 'We cannot all be artists, so what Flaubert knew of how to give dignity and meaning to life was of no value to his fellow man and he never proffered these views on Art in works he published himself.'[39] His conscious intention in the work is to delineate realistically and ruthlessly a society which kills all creative drives. It is Flaubert's theory which James 'sees all round intellectually', a theory which could lead to the sterile aestheticism of a Gilbert Osmond. But something in Emma's vision continues to live on in the reader after Emma is dead, after Charles is dead (perhaps the kind of immortality Virginia Woolf's Mrs Dalloway dreams of, in which she will be diffused into the lives of those she has touched).

As Austen wisely wrote, 'Seldom, very seldom, does complete truth belong to any human disclosure.' In a special sense the ending of *Madame Bovary* is as open as the ending of *Emma*, and Flaubert wrought better than he knew. Emma Bovary is not, finally, a representative of a dying literary school, nor a victim of provincial stupidity; she is a three-dimensional figure, however inconsistent. Flaubert endows her with a vision comparable to his own; her romantic temperament, like his, has a compulsion to seek beauty even when grovelling in the mud. And that beauty is not simply the formal perfection of a work of art, but the less than perfect beauty of the human spirit whose reach, even in the lowliest of human beings – only provided that she be imaginative – must always exceed her grasp.

4

Dorothea Brooke: the Reluctant Aesthete

Since I can do no good because a woman,
Reach constantly at something that is near it.
(Beaumont and Fletcher, *The Maid's Tragedy*, 1619)

'THE SKIRTS OF LIGHT': THE PROVINCIAL HEROINE AS SHAPING FORCE

Middlemarch is probably the finest Victorian novel, by what is arguably the most cosmopolitan and deeply philosophic mind of the period. That that mind also happened to be feminine is reflected in the convictions and fate of George Eliot's great heroine Dorothea Brooke. *Middlemarch* has often been described as the most Tolstoyan of British novels, but actually, as Gordon Haight points out, the influence was the other way around: Tolstoy had probably read *Middlemarch* in translation as he was beginning work on *Anna Karenina*.[1] Unlike Tolstoy's Anna or Flaubert's Emma Bovary, however, who are essentially passive victims, Eliot's Dorothea affords a particularly salutary and moving example of the interaction of micro- and macrocosm, individual and society. Emily Dickinson's image of the poet as David confronting a Goliath-like world ('I took my power in my Hand – / And went against the World – '), while relevant to all our heroines and helpful in defining the tradition to which they belong, can be most poignantly and cogently applied to Dorothea Brooke.[2]

Many readers have felt that, despite Dorothea's ultimately disappointing impact on society, *Middlemarch* is a good, somehow comforting, book to live inside. The dominant metaphor of the novel is Tertius Lydgate's: 'there must be a systole and diastole in all inquiry', and 'a man's mind must be continually expanding and shrinking between the whole human horizon and the horizon of an

81

object-glass'.[3] As David R. Carroll remarks, however, Lydgate himself fails to connect the physiological heart with the spiritual – what Nathaniel Hawthorne called 'the truth of the human heart'.[4] He thus ignores 'the whole human horizon' in favour of the 'horizon of an object-glass'. It is Dorothea, rather than Lydgate, who is most sensitive to the pulsations of the human heart, who transcends egoism in her awareness, however untutored and misguided, of the expansions and contractions, the constant oscillation between 'Me' and 'Not-Me', in all of human existence.

George Eliot is conscious of working in a fictional tradition of creative, imaginative provincial heroines that goes back at least to Charlotte Ramsey Lennox's *The Female Quixote* (1752). In two different letters she speaks of her fondness for reading Jane Austen's *Emma* aloud. Ellen Moers suspects that Austen's lively dialogue may have sparked the clever repartée of the *Middlemarch* world,[5] but I am more interested in the affinities of the two heroines. Whether or not Eliot had read Flaubert's *Madame Bovary* (1857), it was reviewed while she was editor of the *Westminster Review*. Her subtitle, 'A Study of Provincial Life', sounds like an echo of Flaubert's subtitle, 'Moeurs de Province', and both writers filter their visions of provincial life through the eyes of an imaginative heroine.[6] She may well have intended to write an English, and deeply moral, answer to *Madame Bovary*.

The range of her heroine's vision, however, is altogether wider than that of Emma Woodhouse or of Emma Bovary, as the nature of her mistakes is more complex, subtle and varied. 'Romances of chivalry' and 'the social conquests of a brilliant girl', we are told in the Prelude, interest Dorothea Brooke not at all, in contradistinction to the two Emmas. Nor was Eliot to write, as Flaubert did about Yonville after Emma Bovary's horrible death, 'Depuis les événements que l'on va raconter, rien, en effet, n'a changé à Yonville.'[7] Instead, she concludes *Middlemarch* with an affirmation that human progress is largely the product of those anonymous, small, misguided efforts of human beings like Dorothea who, defeated in their original farsighted goals, none the less 'widen the skirts of light' – it is significant that the metaphor is feminine – and make 'the struggle with darkness narrower':

> Her full nature, like that river of which Cyrus broke the strength, spent itself in channels which had no great name on the earth. But the effect of her being on those around her was incalculably

diffusive: for the growing good of the world is partly dependent on unhistoric acts; and that things are not so ill with you and me as they might have been, is half owing to the number who lived faithfully a hidden life, and rest in unvisited tombs.   (p. 613)

The image of all-pervasive fertility, signalled also by her maiden name, Brooke – the name by which we continue to identify her even after her marriage to Casaubon – emerges in sharp contrast to the 'desert' image associated with Emma Bovary, whose cadaver virtually disintegrates into dust before our eyes at the end of the novel.

Major historical events form the backdrop for the important events of Dorothea's life. When she begins her Roman honeymoon with Casaubon, 'George the Fourth was still reigning over the privacies of Windsor', and 'the Duke of Wellington was Prime Minister'. A few months later, 'George the Fourth was dead, Parliament dissolved, Wellington and Peel generally depreciated, and the new King apologetic' (pp. 139, 261). By this time, Dorothea's own illusions about the greatness of her husband's biblical scholarship have been shattered. Disruptions in the state are paralleled to those in Dorothea's private life. But Dorothea's vision, however limited and imperfect, has a greater impact on her immediate circle than the death of a king, the dissolution of Parliament – or even the passage of the First Reform Bill in 1832.

MICROCOSM AND MACROCOSM: THE 'SYSTOLE AND DIASTOLE' OF HUMAN INQUIRY

Dorothea's destiny is the structural, as well as spiritual, centre of this infinitely complex novel. George Eliot once wrote that the subject of 'Miss Brooke' 'has been recorded among my possible themes ever since I began to write fiction'.[8] Miss Brooke's story constitutes the primary plot of *Middlemarch*; the novel is framed, at beginning and end, by interviews between Dorothea and Celia, her 'pink and white nullifidian' younger sister. In the course of the novel, Dorothea's imperfect consciousness must be brought into a meaningful relation – even a collision – with the outside world, if dream is to be nourished and corrected by reality.

Unlike Emma Woodhouse, Dorothea is not a native of the provincial town in which she lives. She resembles, rather, Henry James's Isabel Archer, also an orphan, in that her upbringing has failed to provide her with any real concept of order. Since the age of twelve, she has been raised and educated 'on plans at once narrow and promiscuous, first in an English family and afterwards in a Swiss family at Lausanne' (p. 6).[9] When she marries Casaubon, she mourns because there is not enough for her to do at Lowick, his home: 'she would have preferred, the possibility of finding that her home would be in a parish with a larger share of the world's misery, so that she might have had more active duties in it' (p. 57).[10]

The *données* of Dorothea's predicament can be classified as geographical or spatial, social, educational and sexual. Of these four factors, the last is the most crucial and, in fact, determines the particular character of the other three. In Eliot's novel there is a tension between woman perceived as art object and woman perceived as artist.[11] At times we wonder if woman must first herself be fashioned into work of art, before she can in turn benefit others by becoming an active shaping force. Dorothea is seen as a statue of Ariadne, as a portrait by Naumann, as a perfect crystal, before her influence begins to be felt on Middlemarch, when she supplies an ideal of conduct for both Will Ladislaw and Tertius Lydgate. As Eliot affirms, the 'tragic failure' of the life of such a visionary woman, 'a Saint Theresa, foundress of nothing', is the result of a conflict between the vague aspirations of the inner life, and the mediocrity of the outer (p. 4).

In the first edition of the novel, Eliot wrote a sweeping condemnation of public opinion, represented by the 'lights of Middlemarch', for reinforcing the illusions, unworldliness and ignorance of such women as Dorothea:

> Among the many remarks passed on her mistakes, it was never said in the neighbourhood of Middlemarch that such mistakes could not have happened if the society into which she was born had not smiled on propositions from a sickly man to a girl less than half his own age – on modes of education which make a woman's knowledge another name for motley ignorance – on rules of conduct which are in flat contradiction with its own loudly-asserted beliefs.   (p. 612)[12]

She also alludes to the examples of Antigone and Saint Theresa, and indicates that her primary interest is not simply the perfectibility of society, but the vital role that women, those 'frail vessels of the affections',[13] must play if it is to be perfected. When she claims that 'Miss Brooke' contains a theme she has always had in mind, she tacitly admits that the portion of the novel concerned with *woman's* destiny is closest to her heart.

Eliot herself best expresses the interaction of character and social setting which is the core of her novel. As she once wrote, 'It is the habit of my imagination to strive after as full a vision of the medium in which character moves as of the character itself.'[14] Middlemarch is the 'medium' in which Dorothea moves and has her existence. As such, it shapes her life, particularly through its effects on Lydgate and Ladislaw, even when she is unconscious of its influence. It is also the 'medium' with which she, as artistic figure, has to work and try to shape, even though she may never attain 'as full a vision of the medium' as her creator.

At the beginning of the novel, Dorothea is as wrapped in inner vision as Emma Bovary and knows little of the town in which she has not even been raised. Her vague yearnings have as yet found no medium in which to work. Eliot continually emphasises her shortsightedness, a literal myopia combined with a comprehensive, idealistic inner vision. Both serve to make her overlook the real and near-at-hand. Her ambition is to serve as the 'eyes' for a great Milton going blind, but ironically her own vision is far from perfect and she is all too apt to tread on small animals which get underfoot.

Her sister Celia, on the other hand, has the 'microscopic eye'. Dorothea perceives Casaubon's resemblance to the portrait of John Locke, but Celia notices his 'two white moles with hairs on them' (p. 15). Celia constantly plays Sancho Panza to Dorothea's Don Quixote. Eliot underlines this counterpoint in an epigraph depicting the 'Mambrino's helmet' episode from the Cervantes novel:

'Seest thou not yon cavalier who cometh toward us on a dapple-grey steed, and weareth a golden helmet?' 'What I see,' answered Sancho, 'is nothing but a man on a grey ass like my own, who carries something shiny on his head.' 'Just so,' answered Don Quixote: 'and that resplendent object is the helmet of Mambrino.'   (p. 11)

The 'helmet' turns out to be an inverted barber's basin; but Cervantes, like Eliot, poses the question: which is the superior vision – the Don's idealism, or Sancho's sceptical realism? Similarly, which is superior – Dorothea's inner, idealistic, comprehensive vision, or Celia's satirical eye for human weaknesses and degrading details? In a typical exchange between the sisters, Dorothea, asked what is troubling her, replies, 'Oh, all the troubles of all people on the face of the earth.' The response is, '"Dear me, Dodo, are you going to have a scheme for them?" said Celia, a little uneasy at this Hamlet-like raving' (p. 569).[15]

Dorothea herself is painfully aware of the need to find an 'objective correlative' to her inner vision. She is continually trying to create a dialogue between her comprehensive but vague vision, and the concrete, teeming, but aesthetically and morally formless life of the cottagers, farmers, bankers, lawyers, doctors, clergymen and manufacturers surrounding her. Like Lydgate, she is aware of the systole and diastole in human existence, and tries to impart some beauty and pattern to the life she but imperfectly perceives around her. As a woman, however, her direct participation in that life is restricted to two socially sanctioned forms: (1) marriage, and (2) patronage by means of her wealth and property. If Lydgate, after marriage to Rosamond Vincy, feels his universe 'contracting to a nutshell', Dorothea finds, when she moves to Lowick, that the whole parish is 'contained in a nutshell'. It is hilarious, but at the same time very sad, that after her sacrificial interview with Rosamond Lydgate at the end of the novel, Dorothea can find no outlet for her 'superfluous strength': 'What was there to be done in the village? Oh dear! nothing. Everybody was well and had flannel; nobody's pig had died' (p. 589).

Eliot does, however, make it abundantly clear that Middlemarch is in far greater need of correction from Dorothea's idealism than Dorothea's vision is in need of correction from Middlemarch. Eliot sees English provincial society as sadly deficient in both the moral and the aesthetic senses, which to her, as to Henry James, are inseparable and interdependent.

Dorothea's first encounter with Middlemarch society *en masse* comes only towards the end of Book I, in Chapter 10. With electioneering in his already overstuffed mind, Mr Brooke has extended one of his 'increasingly miscellaneous invitations' to the Grange to a broad spectrum of Middlemarchers, including Bulstrode, the banker; Vincy the mayor, his brother-in-law; Standish the lawyer; and Chichely, the 'coursing celebrity', all standing about 'in duos and trios more or less inharmonious' (p. 65). The musical analogy points up the lack of a sense of aesthetic form in Middlemarch. This aesthetic stupidity prepares us for the failure of the Middlemarchers, in this first great 'gossip' scene, to recognise the superiority of Dorothea's majesty and spiritual beauty to Rosamond Vincy's 'filigree', as Mr Chichely calls it, her 'swan neck' and apparent docility.

Dorothea is aware of her spiritual isolation from her neighbours when she decides to marry Casaubon: 'Dorothea knew of no one who thought as she did about life and its best objects' (p. 36). Yet it is the 'world around Tipton' which has permitted her to make such a disastrous mistake.

George Eliot took the greatest pains with 'Miss Brooke', the first book of her novel. By 1870 she had produced only one hundred pages, and she expressed fears that she was 'refining when novel readers only think of skipping'. In the 'Middlemarch' sections, as well, the focus is on Dorothea, even when she herself is not present. Eliot anticipated Henry James's criticism that the novel is 'a treasure-house of detail, but an indifferent whole'.[16] She affirmed that the book *is* tightly unified, despite, or in fact because of, the four separate threads of the two main plots – concerning Dorothea and Lydgate – and the two secondary – concerning Fred Vincy and Bulstrode: 'I don't see how I can leave anything out, because I hope there is nothing that will be seen to be irrelevant to my design, which is to show the gradual action of ordinary causes rather than exceptional.'[17] Book VII, 'Two Temptations', is the only book in which the Dorothea-plot is not at the heart of the action. Significantly, this is the blackest section of the novel, in which Bulstrode yields to his temptation, and Lydgate is accused of complicity in Raffles's death. In this section Dorothea's 'incalculably diffusive' influence on the lives of others is suggested by the fact that her temporary absence in Yorkshire seems ominous for Lydgate. At the very end of this book, she intuitively, on her return, expresses her faith in Lydgate and prepares us for the 'sunrise' of Book VIII: 'You don't believe that Mr Lydgate is guilty of anything base? I will not believe it. Let us find out the truth and clear him!' (p. 536).

In the 'Lydgate' sections, Dorothea's role remains primordial. Lydgate's fate is parallel to Dorothea's, for he too is a visionary, though in the realm of science, and he too is imprisoned by the mediocrity of Middlemarch. But Eliot indicates that society itself is more at fault in the case of the woman than of the man. As the epigraph of Book I, Chapter 4, reminds us, 'Our deeds are fetters that we forge ourselves', but 'it is the world that brings the iron' (p. 25). Lydgate is more responsible for forging his own fetters than Dorothea.

The story of Lydgate's failures does not merely parallel Dorothea's frustrated creativity. It is, above all, the story of a talented man who fails largely because he makes the initial mistake of refusing to treat woman as 'rational helpmate and companion', to borrow Mr Knightley's terms from *Emma*. His ideal woman is a romanticised fairy princess. For Lydgate a charming, graceful wife, like art and literature, is merely a soothing distraction from the real business of life. Dorothea's initial conception of marriage, on the other hand, totally excludes the notion of romantic love: both marriages are, with equally catastrophic results, founded on illusion. Lydgate's brilliant career is ruined by a silly woman; Dorothea's life is almost stultified by marriage to a man she mistakenly sees as a latter-day Milton or Pascal. It is easy to judge which illusion was the nobler.

There is a wistful thread of a would-be romance, throughout the novel, between Lydgate and Dorothea.[18] Eliot sets up much the same blonde–brunette antithesis between Rosamond and Dorothea that Austen does between Harriet Smith and Emma. There are constant comparisons between Rosamond, the 'huckster's daughter', and the queenly Dorothea. The notion is explicitly stated by Rosamond who, in later life, taunts her husband: 'It was a pity he had not had Mrs Ladislaw, whom he was always praising and placing above her' (p. 610). After Dorothea has expressed her faith in his professional integrity, Lydgate thinks that her love might be more helpful to a man than her financial patronage.

Lydgate *could* have served a similar function to Mr Knightley's in *Emma*: he has the capacity to initiate the heroine into realms of knowledge and experience from which she is excluded by virtue of her provincial isolation and her deficient and anachronistic education (Jeremy Taylor and Pascal replace the *Adelaide and Theodore* which shapes Emma Woodhouse's imagination). Unlike Mr Knightley, however, he has 'spots of commonness' which hinder him from perceiving Dorothea's nobility until it is too late for them to establish intimacy. In the initial 'gossip' scene at Tipton, he tacitly supports the Middlemarch preference for Rosamond and considers Dorothea 'about as relaxing as going from your work to teach the second form, instead of reclining in a paradise with sweet laughs for bird-notes, and blue eyes for a heaven' (p. 70). Thus these two destinies touch momentarily, but never intersect.

'THE LIGHTS OF MIDDLEMARCH'

In a number of key scenes George Eliot affords us a glimpse of 'the lights of Middlemarch', which are unlikely to contribute any new sense of order to Dorothea. In *Madame Bovary*, Flaubert paints Yonville as both cemetery and marketplace, in particular in the 'Comices agricoles' scene. George Eliot's satirical treatment of a provincial funeral and a provincial auction sets up much the same pattern for her 'Study of Provincial Life' that Flaubert does for his 'Moeurs de Province'.

'The Trappings of Woe': a Middlemarch Funeral

Peter Featherstone's funeral takes place in Lowick parish (Lowick is undoubtedly a tag name), where it is witnessed by Dorothea. If she were an artist, her particular bias would be that of the novelist of manners: 'I am fond of knowing something about the people I live among. ... One is constantly wondering what sort of lives other people lead, and how they take things' (p. 238). What Dorothea sees provides a not very heartening foreshadowing of the eventual fate of her own quest for beauty in such surroundings. Middle-march is a *'prosaic neighbourhood'*. Old Peter Featherstone's power drive, 'the rigid clutch of his dead hand' over his earthly wealth, anticipates the later Book v, entitled 'The Dead Hand', in which Casaubon clutches the blooming Dorothea's life from beyond the grave.

Dorothea's poetic sense mourns the funeral as 'a blot on the morning', just as she will later grieve over her husband's refusal of a free gift of love in favour of an authoritarian clasp. Dorothea wants to establish some vital connection between the 'rich Lowick farmers' at the funeral and herself, to include them in her 'lofty conception of the world'. Eliot uses the provincial landscape as the visible embodiment of Dorothea's socially conditioned loneliness and discontent: 'The country gentry of old time lived in a rarefied social air: dotted apart on their stations up the mountain they looked down with imperfect discrimination on the belts of thicker life below. And Dorothea was not at ease in the perspective and chilliness of that height' (p. 238).

Casaubon, unlike Dorothea, has no curiosity about the Featherstone funeral: he slips into the library 'to chew a cud of erudite mistake about Cush and Mizraim', leaving her to observe and interpret alone. By comparing him to a ruminant animal, Eliot suggests that he is on a level with 'the collections of strange animals' who appear at the funeral. Dorothea herself, on the other hand – unlike Emma Bovary at the 'Comices agricoles' – retains a position remote from the prevalent barnyard imagery. She looks down on the funeral from a high window in a scene which can be compared with another famous episode in *Madame Bovary*, that analysed by Jean Rousset in which Emma's 'regard surplombant' on Yonville anticipates her ultimate prostitution and death at the hands of the town. While Dorothea is to become increasingly involved in the life of Middlemarch, she is never, unlike Emma, dragged down to its level.

The Featherstone funeral foreshadows the plot;[19] more importantly, it introduces the twin themes of mortality and inherited wealth. Although Middlemarch is supposedly a healthy spot, much of the novel is concerned with sickness. Even the robust Lydgate dies at the age of fifty of diphtheria, a disease for which he might have discovered a cure had he been strong enough to resist Rosamond. Dorothea's genuine mourning at both the Featherstone and Casaubon funerals is mocked by the image of the dead hand clutching its gold, and Middlemarch, like Yonville, is both marketplace and cemetery.

Art in the Marketplace: a Middlemarch Auction

The name 'Middlemarch' suggests middle-class neutrality, the 'march' perhaps deriving from the French 'marché' or 'market' as well as the English 'marches' or border country. The one 'aesthetic' event Middlemarch celebrates is the auction of Edwin Larcher's furniture, books and pictures. Unlike the strong, silent Caleb Garth, Trumbull the auctioneer's vocation depends on his power of speech, and his 'encyclopaedic knowledge' ('encyclopaedic' meaning simply miscellaneous). Like everyone else in the novel, Trumbull has his private vision of order: he 'would have liked to have the universe under his hammer, feeling that it would go at a higher price for his recommendation' (pp. 441–2). Trumbull represents the spirit of Middlemarch, in which everything is for sale, even the people.[20] Will Ladislaw is a notable exception to this marketability, rejecting in this scene Raffles's advances as he later refuses Bulstrode's offer to buy him off.

Trumbull's qualifications as art critic are ironically illuminated in this scene; he instructs the Middlemarchers as to the cash value they should attribute to the aesthetic. Middlemarch never judged art by its form, structure or technique, but only by theme, frame or extraneous consideration. When cash is the ultimate criterion for taste, the auctioneer must praise 'those things most which were most in want of praise' (p. 445).

'The Uncertainties in Provincial Opinion'

Dorothea is not present at all in this scene, as she was only a distant observer at the Featherstone funeral. She is effectively excluded from active participation in many of these scenes which might otherwise have channelled and directed her energies. She is also excluded from the Middlemarch gossip scenes, even though she and her immediate family and friends are often their subject. Eliot illustrates 'the uncertainties in provincial opinion at that time' by Mr Vincy's reaction to politics: as mayor, he is not clear as to 'whether it were only the general election or the end of the world that was coming on' (p. 261). She characterises 'the lights of Middlemarch' as 'the glow-worm lights of country places'.

François Mauriac has described a French provincial town as 'un désert sans solitude', an apt distillation of Middlemarch as well. There are two principal kinds of gossip scenes in the novel: those of the 'women's chorus' – Mrs Sprague, Mrs Toller, Mrs Hackbutt and Mrs Plymdale – beautifully orchestrated by Eliot, and the plebeian Green Dragon gossips. The women's chorus is the more sanctimonious of the two; concern for a friend's soul calls forth 'remarks tending to gloom, uttered with the accompaniment of pensive staring at the furniture' (p. 543). In Jane Austen's time the middle classes were slowly struggling upward to respectability, but never to an equal footing with the country gentry. In *Middlemarch*, on the other hand, the country gentry is in a ferment of change and new ideas (though often muddled), while the middle classes are striving only to maintain their firmly entrenched position in the closed society which *they* have created.

The Green Dragon gossips have one virtue at least – or perhaps one should say that they lack one vice evidenced by the women's chorus: they make no pretence of an interest in their victims' moral improvement. If they try to create a kind of aesthetic order, unlike Dorothea and Eliot herself, they prefer fantasy to truth, and amorphous, 'fantastic' shapes to the order of nature: 'Bulstrode's earlier life was ... melted into the mass of mystery, as so much lively metal to be poured out in dialogue, and to take such fantastic shapes as heaven pleased' (p. 529). Art, for the town, is 'the superior power of mystery over fact' (p. 524).[21]

The so-called 'lights of Middlemarch', then, are santimoniousness, a drive for power, an enforced mediocrity, an invasion of privacy, a closed society and a transformation of aesthetic and human values into cash.

The Middlemarch Aesthetic: 'Feminine Fine Art'

Whatever aesthetic concern there is in Middlemarch is left to the women, perhaps so that they may use their stored-up energies in activities which do not threaten the dominance of men: 'Women were expected to have weak opinions; but the great safeguard of society and of domestic life was, that opinions were not acted on' (p. 7). As the auction scene indicates, it is primarily the women who are concerned with collecting art and artifacts, but only as status symbols. It is no wonder that Dorothea has complete scorn for the one kind of 'artistic' endeavour she knows, the usual package of 'feminine accomplishments' designed to bait the Venus fly-trap.[22]

Rosamond Vincy, 'the pattern-card of the finishing school', is the ultimate refinement of the Middlemarch aesthetic. Her piano-playing, like her needlework[23] and her acting, is skilled in technique, but imitative, a mere 'echo', not creative. Her art is part of her sexual ammunition, not a gratuitous act.[24]

Dorothea's response to her sister Celia's playing provides an ironic commentary on this particular female accomplishment: 'After dinner, when Celia was playing an "air, with variations", a small kind of tinkling which symbolised the aesthetic part of the young ladies' education, Dorothea went up to her room to answer Mr Casaubon's letter' (p. 33).[25] Eliot herself is in sympathy with Dorothea's apparent 'aesthetic' blindness: Dorothea's 'slight regard for domestic music and feminine fine art must be forgiven her, considering the small tinkling and smearing in which they chiefly consisted at that dark period' (p. 48).

When Middlemarchers turn their critical abilities to the literary productions of Fred and Mary Vincy, they reveal a characteristic scorn for the feminine intellect. Fred writes on the 'Cultivation of Green Crops and the Economy of Cattle-Feeding', and Middlemarch is 'inclined to believe that the merit of Fred's authorship was due to his wife, since they had never expected Fred Vincy to write on turnips and mangelwurzel'. But when Mary writes 'Stories of Great Men, Taken from Plutarch', the authorship is, naturally, attributed to Fred, who has 'been to the University, "where the ancients were studied"' (p. 608).

Rustic Ugliness: Dorothea's Gropings

Like Mary Garth, but without the benefit of Mary's schoolteacher-mother, Dorothea seeks to impart beauty to the mediocrity of the life surrounding her. She rejects the decorative art of a Rosamond Vincy for the supposedly masculine realms of theoretic and practical knowledge. Early in the novel, her gropings have been in the direction of what Caleb Garth refers to as 'business': building or architecture, one form of art which at its best can unite the functional with the aesthetic.

The farmers' lives are not so much impoverished as they are depressing and ugly. Dorothea's cottages are but a first step towards bringing beauty into their lives, and she makes the greatest progress with her architectural plans on Sir James Chettam's estate. Like Thoreau, she realises that a house can grow out of the inner needs of the cottagers, give them an example of beauty and utility to which they can respond.

Caleb Garth pays Dorothea the tribute of admitting that, although a woman, she has 'a head for business' (meaning architecture and scientific agriculture).[26] 'Business' is Caleb's philosophy 'without the aid of philosophers', his 'religion without the aid of theology'. Eliot implies it could also be Dorothea's, had her womanhood not excluded her from a very profound knowledge of this art. Dorothea is aware of her own inadequacy: 'I shall think I am a great architect, if I have not got incompatible stairs and fireplaces' (p. 11).

Not only does she fail to attain a very profound knowledge of architecture, but she is herself imprisoned within the depressing architecture of Lowick, with its 'garden' of funereal and poisonous yew trees and its air of 'autumnal decline' which resembles that of its owner. The lights of Lowick are even dimmer than the lights of

Middlemarch, and Casaubon is preoccupied with a dead past. When Dorothea speaks to him about cottages for the poor, he characteristically, as David Carroll remarks, can think only of the dwellings of ancient Egypt.[27]

Casaubon's 'house of consciousness' has its analogue in his physical dwelling, Lowick. Dorothea finds, in a passage that foreshadows the claustrophobic imagery associated with Osmond in James's *The Portrait of a Lady*, that 'the large vistas and wide fresh air which she had dreamed of finding in her husband's mind were replaced by anterooms and winding passages which seemed to lead nowhither' (p. 145).[28] Casaubon himself is lost in this labyrinthine dwelling of his own mind, 'among small closets and winding stairs' (p. 147). Dorothea's mind, on the other hand, is likened to a 'pure home for Will', where 'he could dwell and be cherished' (p. 286). She is implicitly compared at one point to one of those 'saints with architectural models in their hands' (p. 159).

Despite James's criticism of its structure, Eliot conceives of her novel as a fictional edifice. The relation of part to whole in organic architecture is comparable to Lydgate's theory that the primitive tissues are related to the body 'as the various accommodations of a house are built up in various proportions of wood, iron, stone, brick, zinc, and the rest' (p. 110). Or it can be associated with the joint operation of our passions, which 'do not live apart in locked chambers, but bring their provisions to a common table' (pp. 123–4).

Eliot presents us with two vividly realised pictures of the peasant 'low-life' surrounding Middlemarch.[29] As a female member of the upper class, Dorothea is, once again, not present at either of these scenes which might help to crystallise her perceptions of the peasant needs. The first episode introduces us to Dagley, Brooke's tenant at the ironically named 'Freeman's End', which 'a man was free to quit ... if he chose', but 'there was no earthly beyond open to him' (p. 291). Brooke, we are told, is 'a damned bad landlord', and all too typical of the self-styled reformer who fails to see that charity begins at home.[30] The drunken Dagley's diatribe against his landlord is a living lesson to Brooke on 'the facility with which mortals escape knowledge' despite Dagley's having 'a rector in the twin parish who was a gentleman to the backbone, a curate nearer at hand who preached more learnedly than the rector, a landlord who had gone into everything, especially fine art and social improvement, and all the lights of Middlemarch only three miles off' (p. 291).

In the second of these incidents of 'low-life', the men of Frick are suspicious of the coming of the railway, a suspicion based on ignorance. As old Timothy Cooper remarks succinctly, 'I'n seen lots o' things turn up sin' I war a young 'un – the war an' the peace, and the canells, an' the oald King George, an' the new 'un as has got a new ne-ame – an' it's been all aloike to the poor mon' (p. 408). When the rustics attack his surveyors measuring the land for the railway, Caleb Garth proves the one man capable of dealing with this muddle. Because he has 'no cant at command', he can 'reason with rustics who are in possession of an undeniable truth which they know through a hard process of feeling, and can let it fall like a giant's club on your neatly-carved argument for a social benefit which they do *not* feel' (p. 408).

In an age when women were wrapped, like precious jewels, in cotton wool, the sound of the great world can reach them only at several removes. As in the case of Dagley, their social 'freedom' is purely negative, designed to keep them safe in ignorance and sloth.

'The Road to London'

'The road to London' does not seem to offer a very appealing alternative to Middlemarch mediocrity. London is a magnet for none of the principals in the novel except Rosamond. Trying to change Rosamond's mind is equivalent to what Emily Dickinson, describing gentlewomen, refers to as 'assaulting a plush'. By the end of the novel, Rosamond's dreams are as prettily unyielding as ever: 'There was nothing unendurable now: the debts were paid, Mr Ladislaw was coming, and Lydgate would be persuaded to leave Middlemarch and settle in London, which was "so different from a provincial town"' (p. 552).

George Eliot's own ambivalence towards the traditional London –provincial dichotomy is evidenced in the fates of the three principals: Lydgate, Will Ladislaw and Dorothea.

Lydgate has chosen a provincial setting in which to practise his profession, trusting that it will offer greater freedom for his research. He has already had, in Paris, a taste of the lures and corruptions of the big city. His affair with the actress Laure prefigures his marriage to Rosamond. Both women, in a sense, 'murder' their husbands. Both first names are plant images, 'Laurel' and 'the Rose of the World'. Lydgate refers to Rosamond as his 'basil plant', an image drawn from Keats's poem. Lydgate explains patiently to Rosamond that 'basil was a plant which had flourished wonderfully on a murdered man's brains'. Laure, like Rosamond, is a provincial, from Provence, the old Roman 'Provincia'. Unlike Rosamond, however, she has no love for the city in which she makes her career, and has killed her husband because 'he would live in Paris, and not in my country; that was not agreeable to me' (p. 114). Rosamond 'kills' her husband's brains in order to reach the 'earthly paradise' of London. [31]

After the auction, Will Ladislaw trudges reluctantly along the road to London where he, the 'squyer of lowe degre', may prove himself worthy of Dorothea, 'the king's daughter'. While Will trudges along, Dorothea is carried swiftly past him in a carriage. [32] Dorothea seems an unattainable princess at this point, and 'felt a pang at being seated there in a sort of exaltation, leaving him behind' (p. 465).

After Dorothea and Will finally escape the clutch of Casaubon's 'dead hand', and marry at the end of the novel, they move to London, which is inconceivable to Celia: 'How can you always live in a street?' (p. 601). By the conclusion, the provinces have driven out almost everything that rose above mediocrity and, in so doing, have perpetuated their own lack of brilliance. The only talented survivor in Middlemarch is Caleb Garth, whose gifts are suited to the provincial outlet.

Dorothea's escape from Middlemarch, and particularly from the oppressive atmosphere of Lowick, is figured by the imagery of the novel's climactic love scene between Dorothea and Will (Book VIII, Chapter 83). Dorothea has sometimes failed to see that the outer world is frequently that of Sancho Panza – or of his equivalents within the novel, Celia and Mrs Cadwallader. It is then that she stumbles shortsightedly over the furniture, as when she finds Will and Rosamond in an apparently compromising position.

Two patterns of imagery drawn from Dorothea's surroundings correct and anchor her dream vision. The first, depicting the very real difficulties of Dorothea's predicament, is an image of enclosure: the house at Lowick is a prison or a labyrinth through which Dorothea–Ariadne has to find the thread. The other, usually reinforcing Dorothea's optimism about the essential freedom and beauty of human existence, is drawn from external nature. In the love scene at Lowick the two patterns of imagery coalesce. The epigraph is from John Donne:

> And now good-morrow to our waking souls
> Which watch not one another out of fear;
> For love all love of other sights controls,
> And makes one little room, an everywhere.

Casaubon's influence is finally exorcised, and Dorothea is freed from her 'Bluebeard's Castle'.

The storm without imprisons them within the room, but at the same time liberates them as the emotional storm within merges with the storm viewed through the window. Nature, in the form of two lightning flashes, breaks down the final barriers between them. At the second flash, Dorothea leaps away from the window, where she has looked out on wider but formless ambitions, and grasps at Will, who presents a more humble possibility for order in her life.[33] As the real storm assumes symbolic overtones, and makes 'of one little room, an everywhere', it becomes part of the all-pervasive water imagery whose final meaning is achieved in the last paragraph of the novel.

Despite the satisfactions of Dorothea's role with Will, it does not permit her to originate a new order, but only to complement her husband's activities. She is always troubled by the formlessness of her aspirations, 'by the indefiniteness which hung in her mind, like a thick summer haze' (p. 20). Even Will recognises that 'genius' consists 'in a power to make or do, not anything in general, but something in particular' (pp. 61–2). Especially for a woman, Eliot tells us, 'struggling in the bands of a narrow teaching, hemmed in by a social life which seemed nothing but a labyrinth of petty courses, a walled-in maze of small paths that led no whither, the outcome was sure to strike others as at once exaggeration and inconsistency' (p. 21). In marrying Will, 'she had now a life filled also with a beneficent activity which she had not the doubtful pains of discovering and marking out for herself' (p. 610). Yet her whole being longs for the fulfilment expressed in the epigraph to Chapter 44:

> I would not creep along the coast, but steer
> Out in mid-sea, by guidance of the stars.

Marriage to Will is the ultimate fate not of a foolish Rosamond, but, as Eliot tells us, 'of a nature altogether ardent, theoretic, and intellectually consequent' (p. 21). She is rather like the character in Sherwood Anderson's *Winesburg, Ohio*, who claims that he is a lover who has never found his thing to love.

Dorothea's move to London is not seen as an ideal arrangement. She admits, 'I might have done something better, if I had been better' (p. 601). Most readers would be kinder than she is to herself and would modify the statement: she might have done something better, if her provincial setting had been better, and more receptive to new ideas.

Will, it is true, was 'returned to Parliament by a constituency who paid his expenses', and Dorothea 'could have liked nothing better, since wrongs existed, than that her husband should be in the thick of a struggle against them, and that she should give him wifely help' (p. 611). But George Eliot's thesis is that political action is itself dependent upon and subordinate to the 'unhistoric acts'. Like Emma Woodhouse, Dorothea finds a *métier* as helpmate and companion, but 'Many who knew her, thought it a pity that so substantive and rare a creature should have been absorbed into the life of another' (p. 611). And when Dorothea's son eventually inherits Tipton Grange, he chooses a different path from his father. He prefers not to represent Middlemarch in Parliament, 'thinking that his opinions had less chance of being stifled if he remained out of doors' (p.612). He sounds very much a son of Dorothea. Eliot merely implies what Dorothea's ideal outlet might be: her path is tangential to, but never interlocks with, the paths of Caleb Garth (social commitment) and Tertius Lydgate (science).

PORTRAIT OF DOROTHEA: 'THE CHRISTIAN ANTIGONE'

Although Dorothea does not in any sense paint her own portrait in the novel, as Emma Woodhouse does, she is very far from being the mere passive 'Muse' which Emma Bovary represents. Naumann paints her as Santa Clara, and sees her 'as antique form animated by Christian sentiment – a sort of Christian Antigone – sensuous form dominated by spiritual passion' (p. 141). These traits indicate that she has a vision and a will of her own. She comes close to being an artist in her imagination and perceptions, even inspires works of art, without herself producing a concrete expression of her dreams. Leavis has called Dorothea a dream picture of Eliot as she would have liked to be (physical attractiveness combined with brains?), but I feel certain that Dorothea would envy Eliot, rather than the reverse. It seems to me that Dorothea is what Eliot *could* have become had her early idealism not been corrected, focused, shaped by the novelist's realism; and that a George Eliot is what Dorothea could have become, given the leavening of Romanticism and its aesthetic, a father like Caleb Garth, a balanced, rather than feminine, education.

'THE BROOD OF DESIRE': THE SHALLOWNESS OF ABSOLUTES

Dorothea has at least the advantage, over most of the other characters, of sensing her own limits. Many of the others feel that their private 'solar systems' are all-inclusive, whereas we see them as solipsistic. Dorothea's quest, like Eliot's, is for comprehensiveness and, at the same time, for formal shapeliness.

Eliot warns us early of the dangers of metaphorical thinking: 'we all of us, grave or light, get our thoughts entangled in metaphors, and act fatally on the strength of them' (p. 63). As early as *The Mill on the Floss* (1860), Eliot issues such a caveat. Although a novelist (or perhaps because she is a novelist) she is keenly aware of the limits of language:

> O Aristotle! if you had the advantage of being 'the freshest modern' instead of the greatest ancient, would you not have mingled your praise of metaphorical speech, as a sign of high intelligence, with a lamentation that intelligence so rarely shows itself in speech without metaphor, – that we can so seldom declare what a thing is, except by saying it is something else?[34]

The controlling metaphor of many characters is seen as a projection of his or her own egotism. When Will returns from London and finds his 'familiar little world' shattered, Eliot comments that he is 'in one of those tangled crises which are commoner in experience than one might imagine, from the shallow absoluteness of men's judgments' (p. 587). Men arrive at absolutes easily – too easily, Eliot suggests. The egocentrism of each character's system results in a general lack of adaptability either to the flux of human experience, or to the needs of others who cherish systems of their own.

The Mask of Egoism

Eliot reminds us that images are a mask for egoism: 'We are all of us imaginative in some form or other, for images are the brood of desire' (p. 237). Casaubon, like Featherstone, uses a financial metaphor to describe his myth of power – in Casaubon's case, a dream of conjugal bliss. The result of his egoism is the exceeding narrowness which belies his attempt to find an all-embracing 'Key to All Mythologies'. In reality, he cannot see beyond the most limited horizons and, when asked how he 'arranges' his documents, answers literally, 'in pigeon-holes, partly'. The banker Bulstrode's images are also the brood of his own selfish desires. Lydgate criticises 'the broken metaphor and bad logic of the banker's religion' (p. 508). Eliot delineates skilfully the power of images in corroding Bulstrode's will: 'Raffles dead was the image that brought release' (p. 519).

Each character has a particular image to express his private value system, ranging from Celia's harmless 'trade-unionism of marriage' (comparable to Mrs Elton's in *Emma*), with its cult of motherhood focussing on 'the infant Buddha', to Mrs Waule's 'nest-egg', and Rosamond's fairyland of 'preconceived romance' in which 'it was not necessary to imagine much about the inward life of the hero, or of his serious business in the world' (p. 123). Mrs Cadwallader's Meredithean high comedy excludes most of Middlemarch: 'A town where such monsters abounded was hardly more than a sort of low comedy, which could not be taken account of in a well-bred scheme of the universe' (p. 44). Brooke's equestrian imagery is an all too fitting description of his intellectual vagaries:

> The fact is, human reason may carry you a little too far – over the hedge, in fact. It carried me a good way one time; but I saw it would not do. I pulled up; I pulled up in time. But not too hard. (pp. 12–13)

Metaphorical thinking can anaesthetise one's feelings. Bulstrode's religious and Lydgate's medical metaphors clash and result in a short-circuited dialogue, as do Ladislaw's political metaphors and Lydgate's scientific. Lydgate criticises politics for attempting to find a 'universal cure', using a disease image that reveals his own tendency to assert universal claims for medical science (p. 341).

The Flux of Experience

Eliot agrees with Ralph Waldo Emerson that symbols should be dynamic: 'For all symbols are fluxional; all language is vehicular and transitive.'[35] Emerson sees the poet as superior to the mystic, for the latter 'nails a symbol to one sense, which was a true sense for a moment, but soon becomes old and false'; whereas the poet sees 'the independence of the thought on the symbol, the stability of the thought, the accidency and fugacity of the symbol'.[36]

Referring to Lydgate's possible complicity in Raffles's death, Mr Farebrother makes a remark to Dorothea about the very human state of flux: 'character is not cut in marble – it is not something solid and unalterable. It is something living and changing, and may become diseased as our bodies do' (p. 538).[37]

Eliot implies that her own verbal portrait of Dorothea is superior, because couched in dynamic, breathing language, to any marble statue or portrait by Naumann. Will is unconsciously projecting his own feeling of inadequacy as a painter, but he is also speaking for George Eliot (as he could be for Henry James) when he says to Naumann that for a true 'portrait of a woman', 'language is a finer medium':

> 'Language gives a fuller image, which is all the better for being vague. After all, the true seeing is within. ... As if a woman were a mere coloured superficies! You must wait for movement and tone. There is a difference in their very breathing: they change from moment to moment.'   (p. 142)

'Reason not the Need'

A third important objection of Dorothea's and Eliot's to the fixed and rigid systems of the other characters is their irrelevance to human needs, other than their own. This objection lies behind Dorothea's reluctance to incorporate aesthetics into her own system of order. During her honeymoon, she says, 'in Rome it seems as if there were so many things which were more wanted in the world than pictures' (p. 153). Not just Rome, but the English provinces offend her by the disjunction of aesthetics and life: 'I used to come from the village with all that dirt and coarse ugliness like a pain within me, and the simpering pictures in the drawing-room seemed to me like a wicked attempt to find delight in what is false' (p. 285). Brooke, after all, is the possessor of both the 'Corregiosities' and of the 'picturesque' squalor of Dagley's farm.

'THE OTHER SIDE OF SILENCE': THE 'LOFTY CONCEPTIONS' OF DOROTHEA BROOKE AND GEORGE ELIOT

Unlike her husband, Dorothea is in search of a non-compartmental-ised, non-'pigeon-holed' world vision. She is at one with her creator in seeking to transcend the selfishness and rigidity of single systems. By the end of her honeymoon with Casaubon, Dorothea has already reached awareness of the danger of egocentrism. She wrestles twice with her bad angel of self, and in both cases overcomes it. The first struggle occurs when she learns painfully that Casaubon has 'an equivalent centre of self' to her own; the second, when she recognises the 'otherness' of Rosamond.

When Eliot describes the first struggle, there occurs one of the most often-discussed images in the novel, that of the gigantic udder, which represents the world, at which our ego feeds: 'We are all of us born in moral stupidity, taking the world as an udder to feed our supreme selves.' Dorothea early escapes the charge of moral stupidity:

> Dorothea had early begun to emerge from that stupidity, but yet it had been easier to her to imagine how she would devote herself to Mr Casaubon, and become wise and strong in his strength and wisdom, than to conceive with that distinctness which is no longer reflection but feeling – an idea wrought back to the directness of sense, like the solidity of objects – that he had an equivalent centre of self, whence the lights and shadows must always fall with a certain difference.   (p. 157)

Dorothea's is the same quality of empathy that we have already watched Caleb Garth demonstrate with the rustics.

Images of men walking about padded in the cotton wool of stupidity are continually interwoven dexterously throughout

Middlemarch, and the most important of these almost immediately precedes the udder image:

> That element of tragedy which lies in the very fact of frequency, has not yet wrought itself into the coarse emotion of mankind; and perhaps our frames would hardly bear much of it. If we had a keen vision and feeling of all ordinary human life, it would be like hearing the grass grow and the squirrel's heart beat, and we should die of that roar which lies on the other side of silence. As it is, the quickest of us walk about well wadded with stupidity.
>
> (p. 144)

In other words, 'intelligence' is total empathy, not only with mankind, but with the universe; and it is this which not only Dorothea, but George Eliot herself as a novelist, seeks to attain.

The least egotistical of all the arts is the art of the novel, as Eliot conceives of it. Not content to hold a candle to a mirror and create an artificial arrangement, like Rosamond, she attempts to take the pulse of human nature. In so doing, instead of seeking a single 'Key to All Mythologies', she must present a *series* of egos in collision, use a whole *set* of images, and mythological and literary parallels, each of which expresses only some limited facet of truth.

For these reasons also, George Eliot's presentation of Dorothea emphasises that there is no single key to unlock her character, no single image to capture her essence. Emma Woodhouse is consistently seen as the self-deluded artist who unconsciously paints her own portrait; Emma Bovary as a 'muse in a shop window'. But Dorothea is not simply a latter-day Saint Theresa; she is also a queen; Santa Clara painted by Naumann, Santa Barbara locked in her tower by an ogre of a father – in this case by an ogre of a husband old enough to be her father. She is Saint Catherine, patron saint of spinsters, forced to gaze admiringly at her sister's child, the 'infant Bouddha', and Eve, in quest of the apple of knowledge. When she discovers Will with Rosamond, Dorothea is a Diana who 'had descended too unexpectedly on her worshipper'.[38] Most significantly, she is implicitly compared by Eliot, during the Roman scene, to the flower-like statue of the reclining Ariadne beside which she is standing. Dorothea is also flower-like, but not cold marble, which Eliot feels is too hard and stiff a medium to convey the flux and variety of human experience.

Dorothea is seen by Naumann as 'the most perfect young Madonna', and subsequently Lydgate thinks to himself, 'This young creature has a heart large enough for the Virgin Mary' (p. 563). She is a Desdemona enthralled by the mythological tales of her unlikely Othello, Casaubon; an Ophelia whose marriage, as Mrs Cadwallader comments, is equivalent to going to a nunnery; an Imogene in her purity and innocence. Eliot uses multiple religious, mythic and theatrical parallels to trace the implications of her 'portrait of a lady', thereby escaping any imprisoning single order.

Eliot seeks a total vision, an all-embracing 'aesthetic' which is rather art for humanity's sake than art for art's sake. In a letter, she draws the following parallel between aesthetics and morality:

> On its theoretic and preceptive side, morality touches science; on its emotional side Art. Now the products of Art are great in proportion as they result from that immediate prompting of innate power which we call genius, and not from laboured obedience to a theory or rule; and the presence of genius or innate prompting is directly opposed to the perpetual consciousness of a rule. The action of faculty is imperious, and excludes the reflection *why* it should act. In the same way in proportion as morality is emotional, that it has affinity with Art, it will exhibit itself in direct sympathetic feeling and action, and not as the recognition of a rule. Love does not say 'I ought to love' – it loves. Pity does not say 'It is right to be pitiful' – it pities. Justice does not say, 'I am bound to be just' – it feels justly. It is only where moral emotion is comparatively weak that the contemplation of a rule or theory habitually mingles with its action; and in accordance with this, we think experience, both in literature and life, has shown that the minds which are pre-eminently didactic – which insist on a 'lesson', and despise everything that will not convey a moral – are deficient in sympathetic emotion.[39]

Art is 'moral emotion', the directness of feeling which permits her to sense the 'roar the other side of silence'. She is describing the artist; she could well be describing Dorothea, with her spontaneous, 'direct sympathetic feeling and action'.

Dorothea's second wrestling with the evil angel of self, the famous 'vigil' scene, provides a concrete illustration of this wholeness of vision which Dorothea herself seeks to attain. It begins with her exclamation about Will, 'Oh, I did love him!' The scene is comparable, though much more powerful in effect, to Emma Woodhouse's recognition of her love for Mr Knightley. Coming to terms with her own needs and those of others, Dorothea deploys a wealth of images and allusions. The richness of reference suggests that Dorothea's is a formidable mind which is unwilling to nail ultimate meaning to a particular system of values. Moreover, her inventiveness corresponds to the virtuosity her creator has demonstrated throughout the novel. The allusions are open, rather than fixed and limited; they are drawn from the realms of Nature, the Bible, the prison. The first two imply multiple possibilities for expansion and interpretation; the latter offers the contrasting confinement of the cell.

There is a battle between Dorothea's two images of Will – one as a plant, or as 'the spirit of morning', the other as a 'detected illusion' – which are compared by Eliot to 'two living forms that tore her heart in two, as if it had been the heart of a mother who seems to see her child divided by the sword, and presses one bleeding half to her breast while her gaze goes forth in agony towards the half which is carried away by the lying woman that has never known the mother's pang' (p. 576). The allusion is to the Old Testament judgement of Solomon, and reintroduces the theme of justice and mercy which is so important to the novel. Dorothea's thwarted motherhood, the sterility of her marriage to Casaubon, have been much dwelt upon – but ironically it is Rosamond who is seen as the false mother here, Rosamond whose carelessness, when out riding with Godfrey Lydgate, has cost her a baby she did not really love.[40]

We are constantly reminded of Dorothea's maternal quality, especially through references to the Madonna; it is interesting to note that her attraction to Will is, in fact, partly maternal. This may account for some of his general unsatisfactoriness to many readers as a hero.[41] Since she herself has so much strength, she has little need of it in a husband, but rather of his other qualities – Will's ability to illuminate character, or to 'take impressions' and to feel with other people, his spirit of enjoyment, his awareness of art. Will possesses one other quality which makes him an eminently suitable husband for Dorothea: he is almost as aware as she is of the dangers of self-projection. He has 'dreamy visions of possibilities' with her, but he is too much the idealist to 'live in the scenery' of expectations of her widowhood.

During the vigil Dorothea has courted feeling, and has not feebly sought sympathy or oblivion as Rosamond has: 'she besought hardness and coldness and aching weariness to bring her relief from the mysterious incorporeal might of the anguish: she lay on the bare floor and let the night grow cold around her; while her grand woman's frame was shaken by sobs as if she had been a despairing child' (p. 576). The conflicting images of the vigil are banished in a final catharsis, which results in Dorothea's fellow-feeling for Rosamond: 'It was not in Dorothea's nature ... to sit in the narrow cell of her calamity, in the besotted misery of a consciousness that only sees another's lot as an accident of its own' (p. 577). She is moved to shape another life for the best, to emerge from cotton wool into a world in which, if she cannot hear the squirrel's heartbeat, she can at least hear that of her 'rival':

> But the base prompting which makes a woman more cruel to a rival than to a faithless lover, could have no strength of recurrence in Dorothea when the dominant spirit of justice within her had once overcome the tumult and had shown her the truer measure of things. All the active thought with which she had before been representing to herself the trials of Lydgate's lot, and this young marriage union which, like her own, seemed to have its hidden as well as evident trouble – all this vivid sympathetic experience returned to her now as a power: it asserted itself as acquired knowledge asserts itself and will not let us see as we saw in the day of our ignorance.   (p. 577)[42]

At one point Mary Garth suggests that Farebrother tell a fairy-tale to the Vincy children. As Mary describes the tale, she is implicitly rebuking Fred Vincy for his selfish thoughtlessness. But the tale could be applied to all the egoists in the novel, and bears out the moral implication of the chapter heading from Goldsmith: 'These little things are great to little man.'

The tale concerns 'the ants whose beautiful house was knocked down by a giant named Tom, and he thought they didn't mind because he couldn't hear them cry, or see them use their pocket-handkerchiefs' (p. 470). Mary manages to communicate to Fred a sense of his own blindness to the sufferings of her parents, whose name he has used to back his own foolish extravagance. For Fred the universe has, up to this time, revolved around his own not very lofty conception of himself as an English gentleman, in much the same manner as his sister Rosamond's has revolved around her conception of herself as a fairy princess[43] Each of us needs to be shaken out of his complacency that his own 'solar system' is universally comprehensive, and that he is the centre of not only his own universe, but of everyone else's as well.

Dorothea's great strength is her willingness to penetrate the drives and motives of others, even those underlying Casaubon's stultifying and self-defeating biblical scholarship. Similarly, George Eliot's great strength is her ability to delineate with warmth, tolerance, objectivity and understanding even those 'systems', like Rosamond's and Casaubon's, which are most repugnant to her.

'FRAGMENTS OF HEAVEN': THE AESTHETIC RESOLUTION

Dorothea's triumph is great; she succeeds not only in transcending the egocentrism of single systems, but also in communicating to others – although not in literary language – her faith in the human potential. Her defence of Lydgate, for instance, is characteristic: 'I believe that people are almost always better than their neighbours think they are.' The epigraph to the chapter containing this defence suggests that Dorothea's special kind of 'creativity' resides in her faith in human nature, and her ability to make others live up to that faith:

> Full souls are double mirrors, making still
> An endless vista of fair things before,
> Repeating things behind.[44]

A glance back at the opening scene of the novel may reveal how far Dorothea has progressed beyond moral stupidity by the end. At the beginning she is ill-educated, 'just doesn't know enough', and is, furthermore, ashamed of her emotional response to purely aesthetic enjoyment. Eliot's magnificently sympathetic irony reveals her failings as it plays on the opening exchange between this 'Female Quixote' and her Sancho Panza-like 'unenthusiastic sister' whose 'blonde flesh' suffers much under Dorothea's transcendental longings. Dorothea's reaction to their mother's gems is characteristic of her sensuous and aesthetic reaction to beauty for its own sake: 'She thought of having them often by her, to feed her eye at these little fountains of pure colour.' But her feelings of guilt at her enjoyment would prevent her ever wearing them: 'All the while her thought was trying to justify her delight in the colours by merging them in her mystic religious joy' (p. 10). Her very asceticism, however, is self-deceptive, for the first statement in the novel reveals a principle on which Dorothea has probably been unconsciously acting: 'Miss Brooke had that kind of beauty which seems to be thrown into relief by poor dress' (p. 5). Similarly, the simplicity of her hair style exposes an exceedingly well-shaped head.

Eliot's own vision at this point seems to be that Dorothea's more meaningful role would be, not to ignore beauty, to feel ashamed of it, but to bring it into a complete relationship with the rest of human life. Until she can do so, she will perceive but the 'fragments of heaven' represented by the gems: 'It is strange how deeply colours seem to penetrate one, like scent. I suppose that it the reason why gems are used as spiritual emblems in the Revelation of St John. They look like fragments of heaven' (p. 10).

There is at the beginning of the novel a certain leavening lacking in Dorothea's mentality, a moral intransigence. She feels guilt at the sensuous pleasure of horsemanship – 'she felt that she enjoyed it in a pagan sensuous way, and always looked forward to renouncing it' (p. 7).[45] Paintings and sculpture arouse only feelings of revulsion in her: 'To poor Dorothea these severe classical nudities and smirking Renaissance-Corregiosities were painfully inexplicable, staring into the midst of her puritanic conceptions: she had never been taught how she could bring them into any sort of relevance with her life' (p. 54). As with our other heroines, the deficiencies of Dorothea's particular background account for most of the failings of her creativity. Her great quality, like that of Emma Woodhouse and of Emma Bovary, is her womanliness, her capacity for enjoyment and vitality, which, properly channelled, would permit her to feel for and with others and to articulate their sufferings. But they are taught by romantic fiction to see heroines as ethereal and languishing, and Dorothea has been taught a rigid morality by puritanical poems and essays, a morality which she must strive to modify in the course of the novel if she is to bring enjoyment, both aesthetic and emotional, into 'relevance with her life'.

Early in the novel Dorothea has been given insufficient guidance to escape the theological impasse, and is at best a 'reluctant' – even unwilling – 'aesthete', with an exceedingly puritanical knowledge derived from reading Hooker, Pascal, Milton, Jeremy Taylor. To a certain extent Dorothea's plight was also, at one time, Eliot's own. Eliot presents us with a heroine who is to all appearances treading the same path as herself, only forty years earlier.[46] Eliot began her career with a burning interest in the German higher criticism, which she hoped would provide her with a sufficiently 'lofty conception of the universe', and translated Strauss's *Das Leben Jesu*. Only later did she seem to see this interest as not ultimate, and turned first to literary criticism, then to writing novels as the most nearly all-embracing task.

Dorothea does, like her creator, progress beyond the theological impasse by the end of the novel; she is by that time not so reluctant an aesthete, as evidenced by her marriage to Will. From this union Dorothea learns to temper her sense of duty with enjoyment of life, of formal and emotional beauty; Will learns to temper his dilettant-ism with a sense of duty. Yet Dorothea's progress is not so completely satisfactory as many readers, and probably Eliot herself, might wish for her.

Eliot's gentle irony of the opening scene remains consistent to the end. Great as Dorothea's progress is, it cannot lead to a complete transformation of her character. She never quite reaches the level of consciousness of her creator, much less the ability to articulate her perceptions. The irony is necessarily muted during the painful marriage to Casaubon, and during the vigil scene. But it plays on the ridiculous in Dorothea's schemes for a Utopian community in England, and Will's for one in the Far West. It plays on the scene in which Dorothea works on political economy 'to keep her mind steady' after the interview with Rosamond, and on her study of maps because 'a map was a fine thing to study when you were disposed to think of something else, being made up of names that would turn into a chime if you went back upon them' (pp. 589–90). This episode demonstrates, first, Dorothea's instinctively poetic response to weighty learning, and, second, her willing abandon-ment of books (like Isabel Archer's) when life beckons. Chiefly Eliot's irony plays on the love scene when Dorothea happily forgets all her grandiose projects and childishly envisions household economy in terms of her characteristically simple taste in clothes: 'We could live very well on my own fortune – it is too much – 700 a year – I want so little – no new clothes – and I will learn what everything costs' (p. 594).

What renders Dorothea most sympathetic to the reader is that, as her 'education' through experience progresses, she learns to regard her own foibles with something resembling Eliot's own humour and detachment. Dorothea is actually self-critical from the very begin-ning, whereas Emma Woodhouse only develops such a capacity in the course of the novel, after being amused first by everyone's foibles *but* her own. Dorothea does, however, resemble Emma in that she redirects wit and sarcasm aimed at others towards humour and easy tolerance aimed at herself as well.

In the first scene, for instance, her wit is exercised on the 'nullifidian' Celia, who has asked her if she will wear the gems in company: 'Perhaps,' Dorothea replies, 'rather haughtily', 'I cannot tell to what level I may sink.' And Eliot comments, 'Across all her imaginative adornment of those whom she loved, there darted now and then a keen discernment, which was not without a scorching quality. If Miss Brooke ever attained perfect meekness, it would not be for lack of inward fire' (pp. 10–11). By the end of the novel, however, Celia's barbs no longer prick. When she analyses profoundly Dorothea's motives for marrying Will – 'I suppose it is because you must be making yourself uncomfortable in some way or other' – we are told, 'Dorothea laughed' (p. 601).

Dorothea is wiser and more subtle than Emma Woodhouse, because she is aware throughout that she has never found an adequate shaping principle. She is the one major potential artist in the novel, as Naumann, who sees himself as a mere hook or claw through which the universe is straining towards expression, is the one real artist. But, however great her influence for good over the lives of others, it is somehow intangible, and her voice never really finds its unique mode of expression.

If she ever attempts to play God in Middlemarch, as Emma did in Highbury, it is only before life begins to impinge on her consciousness, and with a mere puppy at that: 'The objectionable puppy was thus got rid of, since Miss Brooke decides that it had better not have been born' (p. 22). Her satisfaction is incomplete in the fact that she, like Emma, 'presided in the uncle's household, and did not at all dislike her new authority' (p. 8). Later in the novel, also, Sir James Chettam thinks that she should have been a queen, with an entire kingdom to rule; others see her as the 'queenly young widow', and she 'reigns' in Will's heart. But neither at the beginning nor at the end does she find a goal as worthy as the moral power she could direct towards it. She is not Emma Woodhouse satisfied with being queen in Highbury; she recognises that she is a queen without a kingdom.

She is constantly relegated to the passive role, as clear mirror for others, or as art object. Will, for instance, compares her to a perfect crystal, unlike Rosamond, who is a flawed crystal which at one moment he thinks of shattering.[47] Will also sees her as a poem, rather than a poet:

> 'To be a poet is to have a soul so quick to discern that no shade of quality escapes it, and so quick to feel that discernment is but a hand playing with finely-ordered variety on the chords of emotion – a soul in which knowledge passes instantaneously into feeling, and feeling flashes back as a new organ of knowledge.' 'But you leave out the poems', said Dorothea. 'I think they are wanted to complete the poet. I understand what you mean about knowledge passing into feeling, for that seems to be just what I experience. But I am sure I could never produce a poem.' 'You *are* a poem ...', said Will.   (p. 166)[48]

Eliot defines Art as the power to make readers or spectators 'better able to imagine and to feel the pains and the joys' of others. It is in this power that Dorothea's greatness lies, but she is never permitted to adventure actively on life. Dorothea would prefer to be the creator and not the creation, but with humourous detachment she realises that this can never be, for the poems are needed to complete the poet. This discussion also, more obviously, rebounds on Will's dilettantism: he is likely, unlike Dorothea, to adopt the pose of the artist and interest himself in the creative process to such an extent that he neglects to produce a concrete work.

Dorothea's relation to art is to constantly remain in the conditional category: '*If* I were to write a book', or 'paint a picture', or 'compose music', is her perpetual and humble refrain. We have been tracing several of the causes for her failure to fulfil herself as artist, perhaps even to realise fully that such a role *would* provide fulfilment. Her puritanical background, which has developed the moral sense at the expense of the aesthetic, her failure to find a union of moral and artistic beauty in the mediocre provincial society which surrounds her, her want of guidance from either her family or a strong hero–teacher – all contribute to keep her imagination pinned to earth, to the small and useful tasks which may have an 'incalculably diffusive' effect, but one which will fall far short of her original aspirations.

Perhaps most crucial, for it continues to operate even after the other deficiencies in her background and training have been partially alleviated, is her subjection to a man's world and its values.

A man has at least the *opportunity* of understanding and exploiting the aesthetic experience. The dilettantish Will, the leaky-minded Brooke, like Léon Dupuis, can dabble in poetry, politics, art; but a gifted woman cannot. If a man fails to connect formal beauty with the practical and moral side of existence, it is largely his own fault. Lydgate, for instance, who *has* read Swift, decides that books are 'stuff', and only science will answer the need for unifying experience.[49] His aesthetic blindness is wilful, while Dorothea's is largely conditioned by others. And it is this blindness which makes him see woman as only the 'warrior's plaything', eventually leading him to prostitute his talent for material success.

Dorothea knows her own ignorance, as he does not know his; she sees masculine knowledge initially as a 'height', 'a standing-ground from which all truth could be seen more truly' (p. 47).[50] She is not to be blamed for this assumption, based like Emma Woodhouse's contrary assumption of *feminine* superiority on total inexperience of men. Sir James Chettam's lordly assessment of the relative advantages of the sexes is the dominant one: 'A man's mind – what there is of it – has always the advantage of being masculine, – as the smallest birch-tree is of a higher kind that the most soaring palm, – and even his ignorance is of a sounder variety' (p. 16). This would be amusing were it not for the grave consequences for Dorothea. The great organ at Freiberg makes Dorothea 'sob', and men tell this women, whose soul vibrates to the union of emotion and form, that she is 'to take things more quietly'.[51]

Eliot herself recognises that none of us ever achieves more than a fragmentary vision. At the end of the novel she makes a statement which distinctly echoes Dorothea's about the 'fragments of heaven'. In her 'Finale' she writes: 'Every limit is a beginning as well as an ending. ... For the fragment of a life, however typical, is not the sample of an even web (p. 607).[52] Eliot can, however, at least articulate her fragmented view.

Dorothea recognises that the original impetus for literary creativity must, for her, proceed from deep feeling rather than knowledge: 'if she had written a book she must have done it as Saint Theresa did, under the command of an authority that constrained her conscience' (p. 64). Eliot would agree that this can be the only source of inspiration. But Dorothea does not at this point recognise that lack of knowledge prevents her from giving *form* to the great feeling; the world surrounding her has failed to provide her with the objective correlative to high aspirations and emotions.

Eliot herself has been able to live in a 'man's world' to the extent that she has acquired considerable knowledge of science and of Caleb Garth's 'business' as well as of literature. She is therefore able to give voice to at least a partial vision of the human potential. In Dorothea she presents a portrait of a lady whose lot is the more common one, however great her gifts, and in this George Eliot, like Jane Austen, recognises that her own outlet is extraordinary and that most women are not so privileged. Nevertheless, Dorothea, for all her failures, participates to a surprising degree in her creator's perceptions. In fact, so fully does Dorothea share that vision that the ending *must* be open, and her creative drive must be as tenacious and persistent as that of her predecessors, Emma Woodhouse and Emma Bovary, and her successor, Isabel Archer. Henry James's moving description of Dorothea is to haunt him as he creates his own 'portrait of a lady': 'we seem to look straight into the unfathomable eyes of the beautiful spirit of Dorothea Brooke. She exhales a sort of aroma of spiritual sweetness, and we believe in her as in a woman we might providentially meet some fine day when we should find ourselves doubting of the immortality of the soul.'[53]

5

Isabel Archer: the Architect of Consciousness

---

let our houses first be lined with beauty, where they come in
contact with our lives, like the tenement of the shell-fish, and not
overlaid with it. But, alas! I have been inside one or two of them,
and know what they are lined with.

(Henry David Thoreau, *Walden*, 1854)

'EMMA'S DAUGHTERS': JAMES'S VARIATION ON THE THEME

Henry James has the advantage of building upon a 'small tradition'
served variously by Austen, Flaubert, and Eliot before him, and is
therefore the most conscious of his heroine's literary lineage. In his
Preface to the New York Edition of *The Portrait of a Lady* he quotes
George Eliot (from *Daniel Deronda*) on the importance, in literature
as in life, of 'the Isabel Archers, and even much smaller female fry':
'In these frail vessels is borne onward through the ages the treasure
of human affection.'[1] He compares his Isabel to some of Shakespeare's witty heroines, but especially to Eliot's Hetty Sorrel, Maggie
Tulliver, Rosamond Vincy and Gwendolen Harleth. As George
Levine has also noted, however, the one Eliot heroine closest in
conception to Isabel, Dorothea Brooke, is conspicuous by her
absence.[2]

James wrote essays on all three of his predecessors, but the most
direct evidence is of his debt to Flaubert and Eliot. He praised the
perfections of Flaubert's technique, and admired Emma Bovary's
absorption 'in romantic intention and vision while fairly rolling in
the dust'.[3] But he complained that the heroine's consciousness was
'really too small an affair' to carry the weight of this most crafted of
novels.[4] On the other hand, he felt that *Middlemarch* was 'a
treasure-house of detail', but 'an indifferent whole'.[5] Its virtues

would have been highlighted, he believed, if the magnificent heroine, Dorothea, 'that perfect flower of conception', had been made the centre of the work.[6] His *Portrait* is an attempt to combine the strengths of the French and English novels while avoiding their weaknesses.

In an unusual precautionary warning to the reader, James, as we have seen, protected his heroine from the reader's 'scientific criticism'.[7] Isabel – along with her fictional 'sisters', Emma Woodhouse, Emma Bovary and Dorothea Brooke – is not only a major nineteenth-century forerunner of the contemporary New Woman in quest of a freedom she is not always able to define; she is also an *artiste manqué*. Although she is destined never to produce a concrete work of art, her creator identifies closely with her, as Austen, Flaubert ('I am Madame Bovary') and Eliot did with their heroines. Dorothea Brooke's interest in biblical scholarship traces the same curve of idealism and disillusionment as Eliot's own in her youth. Similarly, Isabel Archer's aunt, Mrs Varian, spreads the rumour that her niece is a budding author, 'Mrs Varian having a reverence for books' (p. 52). While her aunt's notion is ridiculed, James does use his heroine's plight to reflect on certain aspects of his own aesthetic creed and to reveal his own ambivalence about the artist's role in a materialistic society. By the end of the novel, Isabel has erected a fine 'architecture of consciousness' which projects important aspects of her creator's attitude towards art, and which mirrors James's own 'House of Fiction', the central metaphor of both Preface and novel – which not coincidentally takes place in a series of fictional houses charged with symbolism.

In the Preface James credits Turgenev with having suggested the analogy between architecture and novelistic structure, and some critics have compared James's heroines to the Russian novelist's. But Isabel's situation and psychology seem closer to those of Eliot's Dorothea than to Turgenev's characters. Both girls are courted early in their respective novels by English noblemen, Sir James Chettam in *Middlemarch*, Lord Warburton in *Portrait*; neither is much tempted. James paints a verbal portrait of Isabel; Dorothea is painted as a saint by Naumann in Rome. Dorothea's disillusioning Roman honeymoon prefigures Isabel's marriage to Gilbert Osmond and incarceration in the dungeon-like Roman palace, the Roccanera. For both women, Rome is the place where others have suffered and survived.

Even the architectural motif could have been suggested by Eliot. Edward Casaubon's labyrinthine psyche has its physical counterpart in his home, Lowick (Low wick?) where the blooming Ariadne–Dorothea is imprisoned with her Minotaur. Isabel is entombed in the Roccanera (black rock), the house where no flower can grow. Casaubon's mind and Osmond's (the two names have the same hollow reverberation) are both described in architectural terms. Dorothea realises that 'the large vistas and wide fresh air which she had dreamed of finding in her husband's mind were replaced by anterooms and winding passages which seemed to lead nowhere'.[8] Osmond's 'beautiful mind', Isabel learns, is 'the house of darkness, the house of dumbness, the house of suffocation' (p. 353). If Isabel creates an elaborate architecture of consciousness, moreover, Dorothea's one 'artistic' accomplishment is designing cottages for the poor, and she is even seen as a saint with an architectural model in her hand.

In his 1873 review of *Middlemarch*, James claimed that 'Dorothea was altogether too superb a heroine to be wasted',[9] an oversight he seeks to rectify in his own *Portrait* by placing 'the centre of the subject in the young woman's own consciousness' (Preface, p. 10). This central consciousness, whose complexity 'was naturally of the essence' (Preface, p. 11), herself comes to be viewed architecturally: 'this single small corner-stone, the conception of a certain young woman affronting her destiny, had begun with being all my outfit for the large building of *The Portrait of a Lady*. It came to be a square and spacious house ... but, such as it is, it had to be put up around my young woman while she stood there in perfect isolation' (Preface, p. 8).

James associates both heroines with natural as well as architectural imagery, with outdoors as well as indoors. The heroine of *Middlemarch*, he wrote, is 'framed for a larger moral life than circumstance often affords, yearning for a motive for sustained spiritual effort and only wasting her ardour and soiling her wings against the meanness of opportunity'.[10] The flight imagery is recapitulated in *Portrait* by Ralph in particular, who complains that Isabel has been brought to earth by a mere faded rosebud. James stressed, in his review, Dorothea's flower-like quality and 'aroma of spiritual sweetness'.[11] Isabel is seen to unfold gradually, like a flower, and Ralph warns her not to force her growth, as though she were 'trying to pull open a tight, tender young rose' (p. 189).

THE WEDDING OF TWO CULTURES

In Isabel and Dorothea (as in the two Emmas) the dissimilarities are at least as significant as the resemblances. The outlet each heroine finds reflects important differences in English, French and American provincial societies: matchmaking for Emma Woodhouse, adultery for Emma Bovary, social concern for Dorothea Brooke, and for Isabel Archer the creation of a complex structure out of her fine perceptions.

Unlike the other two heroines, however, Isabel's fate is shaped by two distinctly different cultures. She is an American provincial (as for James all Americans are in Europe) transplanted to an alien society, and her portrait is painted against both European and American backgrounds.[12] By the same token, the architecture in the novel ranges from the provincial house in Albany belonging to Isabel's grandmother; to Gardencourt, that almost ideal English–American blend of indoors and outdoors, of form and morality; to Lockleigh, the English nobleman's seat with its romantic moat; to the sinister continental fortresses – the Crescentini, inhabited by the unlikely, insensitive Mrs Touchett; Osmond's mask-like Florentine villa; and, finally, the Roccanera itself.

Isabel has been seen, by Philip Rahv among others, as an American Transcendental heroine.[13] This view would suggest that there is a philosophic, and perhaps aesthetic, dimension to her quest. But James describes extremely limited parameters for the creativity of an ill-taught woman who is at times driven to conform to social expectations of the woman's role. She is, moreover, a Transcendental heroine who must confront (or affront) her fate in Europe. Madame Merle, not usually a trustworthy source, does express a bitter truth of the novel when she exclaims that American women adapt better to Europe than American men because 'a woman, it seems to me, has no natural place anywhere; wherever she finds herself she has to remain on the surface and, more or less, to crawl' (p. 168). All the women in the novel, including Isabel, are seeking some form of self-expression, but their search for an 'art' is finally translated (and often debased) into a search for a home and furnishings. For some the household becomes a kind of aesthetic 'contre-univers', as Gaston Bachelard calls it; for others it merely comprises material possessions.

It is, moreover, no accident that James has seen fit to attach his famous Preface concerning the 'House of Fiction' to a novel whose action takes place in houses which are almost personified as emanations of their indwellers.[14] An analysis of the links between and among three crucial elements – Transcendentalism, the role of women and architecture – may shed some new light on the novel and help to set it in both a European and an American perspective.

James seems to be working towards a wedding of the two cultures from the time of *Madame de Mauves* (1874) and *The American* (1877) through *The Portrait of a Lady* (1881) to the last completed novel, *The Golden Bowl* (1904).[15] The first two end in a dying fall, and only Maggie Verver in *The Golden Bowl*, confronted with European deception, does not renounce all else in favour of the life of fine perception.

Isabel's is not, however, an American–European union, strictly speaking, like the other three, but a marriage between two Americans, one of whom happens to be Europeanised. The very point about Osmond and Madame Merle is that they have adopted European manners without understanding their substance and underlying rationale. James uses the various houses which Isabel visits or inhabits to symbolise the conflict between Isabel's Transcendental idealism and Merle's and Osmond's materialistic realism. At the beginning of the novel, Isabel is the Transcendental innocent who refuses any interest in the world of objects, while Madame Merle and Osmond, at the opposite pole, are exclusively preoccupied with 'things'; they are collectors, not artists. Their drive towards worldly values is never for a moment deflected, and they are unable to see beyond the emptiness of European forms. Isabel, to the contrary, comes to appreciate both the form and the essence of Europe through the series of houses in which her perceptions are sharpened. She increasingly hones and refines her ability to read the nature of the indweller from the exterior and interior of his or her house.

The House in Albany: American Provincialism

For many readers the image of young Isabel Archer shut off from the world in the 'office' of her grandmother's house in Albany epitomises the imaginative provincial heroine. In this setting all the key motifs and images of the book coalesce. Although Isabel has, in fact, lived in New York City and travelled in Europe with her artistic father, her spiritual home is the old house in provincial Albany. Her upbringing is similar to that of Eliot's Dorothea, also an orphan, in that it has failed to provide her with any contemporary concept of order. For both Dorothea and Isabel, the initiation into life and the shaping of character have been dangerously postponed. Before his death, Isabel's father merely carried her in his wake around the Bohemian fringes of Europe and America, never permitting her to put down roots. The result is Isabel's illusion that she can, in an Emersonian sense, 'build therefore [her] own world'; that her choices are completely free, and she is adventuring on life. The English girl, lacking the American faith that the world has infinite possibility, looks back towards a Puritan mysticism completely anachronistic in the 1830s. At the same time, Dorothea senses a gap in her life and seeks self-expression within the framework of a 'coherent social faith and order which could perform the function of knowledge for the ardently willing soul'.[16]

The house in Albany provides an architecturally ideal setting for Isabel's notion of total freedom. As Leon Edel has noted, its description is based on James's own childhood memories.[17] Isabel especially seeks the 'mysterious melancholy' of 'the office' whose seclusion sets free her imagination, even as it limits her perception of external reality.[18]

Her isolation has been in part imposed on her from without, but it is also a matter of her own choosing. Her physical withdrawal, coupled with her imaginative adventurousness, remain constant traits of her character throughout her later explorations of the 'region of delight or of terror' which she equates with Europe. In the 'office' she has no wish to view 'the vulgar street' beyond the blocked door and, like a female Quixote, prefers the company of books. Among her readings are the works of Robert Browning and of the philosophic and idealistic George Eliot, whose Dorothea Brooke she so clearly resembles. Most significantly, she is giving her mind 'marching orders and it had been trudging over the sandy plains of a history of German thought' – doubtless, at that period, including German Transcendentalism. Thus, within a provincial architectural framework, with the aid of readings in Transcendental thought, James's heroine is trying to shape her ideal of personality.

Portraits and Houses

Despite its importance to our understanding of Isabel's childhood and girlhood, the Albany scene is presented only in flashback, and the first artistic analogy we encounter in the novel is not to architecture but to portraiture. James, however, highlights the architecture even in the portrait scenes; for every portrait must have a setting and a frame. James's portraiture is largely expository and presents an objective view of Isabel; in the architectural scenes Isabel is usually the perceiver, not the perceived. We move inside her consciousness, and the experience becomes visceral. At the outset of her adventures, Isabel is avowedly not concerned with houses. Even the Albany house is no exception, for James's description provides no specificity of detail, but rather an impression of the first 'arch' in the novel, the 'tunnel', of space where Isabel's imagination can soar unchecked.

The novel contains at least two portraits of Isabel (as compared to the multiple 'portraits', real and imagined, of Dorothea): one, an early rough sketch of her potential; the other, a later 'portrait of a gracious lady' (Dorothea was described as 'the pattern of a lady'). Isabel is not initially a portrait of a lady; when we witness her dramatic entrance at Gardencourt at the beginning of the novel, ready to seize upon life as fearlessly as she scoops up Ralph Touchett's little terrier, Bunchie, she is at the most a sketch of an unrealised promise. She *becomes* the portrait of a lady only after the marriage to Gilbert Osmond when, through suffering, she develops a kind of queenliness. James reinforces the effect of portraiture by introducing Isabel to us in her two major roles through the eyes of an 'outsider'. Our first glimpse of her *inner* life has to await the Albany flashback.

At the beginning of the novel, it is Lord Warburton, visiting Gardencourt, who declares her to be his 'idea of an interesting woman'. Her essential features are mobility, vivacity, confidence, the ability to take impressions, acute perception, and 'a comprehensiveness of observation' (p. 28). These qualities suggest her potential creativity, rather than any likelihood that she will herself become 'artifact', work of art.

Later in the novel, after the marriage to Osmond, we first see her through the eyes of Ned Rosier: 'framed in the gilded doorway, she struck our young man as the picture of a gracious lady' (p. 303). For both entrances she is dressed in black; for both she is somehow 'framed', placed against a background that sets off her own nature. But there the resemblance ends, for James's symmetrical arrangements points out the vivid contrast between the young American girl ecstatic with vague, unrealised dreams and aspirations, who 'hoped there would be a lord; it's just like a novel!' (p. 27), and the still young, but cosmopolitan and sophisticated matron who has learned 'to take things more quietly'.

It is scarcely possible to think of Isabel's search for an art without visualising her first appearance in the mellow, late afternoon light of civilised Gardencourt, the first frame for her portrait. Gardencourt seems at peace with itself; it is the epitome of a leisured English society which the Touchetts, father and son, have adopted. They have achieved there a delicate balance of two opposing forces: respect for tradition and formal beauty, and openness to the winds of change. At the beginning of the novel, the Touchetts and Lord Warburton are discussing contemporary English political and social issues. Whereas George Eliot gives full attention to such concerns as the medium in which her heroine has her existence, James leaves them on the level of idle small talk at afternoon tea. He does, however, imply that it is the American Touchetts, and not Warburton, who have learned to fuse tradition and innovation, an American moral outlook and a European sense of form.

As its name suggests, Gardencourt embodies an almost ideal blend of house and garden, of outdoors and indoors. It is also a court for the new American 'royalty'. The lawn seems 'but the extension of a luxurious interior'. The trees are likened to 'velvet curtains', and the lawn is 'furnished, like a room, with cushioned seats, with rich-coloured rugs, with the books and papers that lay upon the grass' (p. 18).

It is appropriate that Isabel's first vision of Gardencourt is external, for her imagination at this point is seen not in architectural terms, but as a landscape: 'Her nature had, in her conceit, a certain garden-like quality ... which made her feel that introspection was, after all, an exercise in the open air' (p.55).[19]

Several critics have seen the lawn at Gardencourt as Edenic, but actually only Isabel's garden of introspection should be described in such terms. At first the world seems to her to be that of Eden before the Fall, 'a place of brightness, of free expansion, of irresistible action' (p. 53). But James subtly signals that the world is fallen, and, like his mentor Nathaniel Hawthorne, in most ways he believes that the fall is fortunate. Thus there is a serious deficiency in Isabel's consciousness at the beginning of the novel, for her artistry consists primarily of cultivating the garden of her own nature. Her spontaneity resembles Dorothea Brooke's, but Dorothea's intro- spection is less obviously egocentric, for she is preoccupied with others less fortunate than herself. Isabel, in contrast, is reluctant to remind herself that 'there were other gardens in the world than those of her remarkable soul', as well as some (like the Roccanera) 'which were not gardens at all – only dusky pestiferous tracts, planted thick with ugliness and misery' (p. 55). From time to time Isabel wonders, 'What should one do with the misery of the world in a scheme of the agreeable for one's self?' But, James comments, 'It must be confessed that this question never held her long' (p. 56). When Osmond marries her, he twists and perverts her metaphor for her own consciousness: 'Her mind was to be his – attached to his own like a small garden-plot to a deer-park. He would rake the soil gently and water the flowers; he would weed the beds and gather an occasional nosegay' (p. 355).

The young Isabel's early responses to Gardencourt are in drastic need of the corrective she receives in the course of the novel. She has at the outset an unlimited faith in her own potential for achievement, although she has no idea of the form it will take. Richard Gill is correct in saying that 'Of all the country houses in James, Gardencourt is perhaps the closest to the ideal',[20] but it is important to remember that it cannot *be* ideal. The point is not that it is an English country house, as Gill labels it, but that it represents a fusion of two cultures in that it is owned and modified by Americans. Lord Warburton's Lockleigh, which Gill ignores, is the purely English dwelling in *The Portrait*. Gill is mistaken, too, in seeing Gardencourt as both the 'palace of art' and the 'house of life',[21] because it is, more significantly, the 'house of death' – at least for the invalid Ralph, if not for Daniel Touchett who simply dies of old age. The physical frailty of Ralph, the heir to Gardencourt but already a dying man at the beginning of the novel, strikes a deeply ambiguous note. One wonders if the American who lives abroad yet remains at heart American is somehow deprived of his life sustenance. Yet it is Ralph's frailty and renunciation of the active life which provide Isabel – through whom he can experience vicariously – with the substance to feed her imagination. At the same time, Ralph makes Isabel an easy victim of the kind of attraction exercised by Gilbert Osmond. In the Gardencourt scenes we become aware that Isabel, contrary to her own protestations, will need to accept material aid if her dreams are ever to be connected with reality. Her fictional 'sisters', already analysed, share her uneasy relationship to inherited wealth. That Emma Woodhouse is an heiress defines her character, but also imprisons her in her father's house. Emma Bovary is poor but extravagant and Dorothea Brooke is controlled by

Casaubon from beyond the grave by her inheritance from him, and its conditions.

Only in the house in Albany is Isabel 'free' – to dream, but not to act. At Gardencourt Isabel begins to perceive the restrictions imposed by her womanhood, as well as those imposed by her relative inpecuniousness. Gardencourt is only partly a liberated American abode; it also observes the strict decorum of 'decent houses' in Europe. Isabel's aunt warns her that she must not stay up with the men unchaperoned: 'Young girls here – in decent houses – don't sit alone with the gentlemen late at night' (p. 66).[22] Isabel obeys the custom of the country somewhat reluctantly, almost wishing herself back in her 'blest Albany'. But she turns her aunt's lesson to good use as the first step in her European education and asserts that she intends, in her womanly way, to continue exercising her free will:

> 'I always want to know the things one shouldn't do.'
> 'So as to do them?' asked her aunt.
> 'So as to choose', said Isabel.   (p. 67)

Daniel Touchett claims that, in the face of social change, 'The ladies will save us' (p. 23), but Isabel immediately begins to learn that her scope for action will be very limited. Even the enlightened Ralph reiterates that the only true freedom for women exists in marriage, not outside it. When Isabel affirms, 'I don't want to begin life by marrying. There are other things a woman can do', Ralph gently chides her, 'There's nothing she can do so well' (p. 132).

By the time we meet Isabel in her new role as 'Mrs Osmond', her energies have been muted, and the setting is no garden, but the claustrophobic Roccanera. James intimates that there have been corresponding gains and losses in her situation since our first view of her. Her aesthetic gain as suitable subject for a finished portrait is counterbalanced by her loss of possible outlets for creativity. It is true that the art of portraiture demands a certain passivity, or an arrested attitude, on the part of the sitter. Isabel has found her special niche or role. She has doubtless learned the lesson that 'genius' consists not in doing everything in general (in the manner of Emma Woodhouse, the would-be Leonardo da Vinci of High-bury), but rather in doing something in particular. Most readers, however, are inclined to question the worth of the 'something in particular' she has chosen to do in marrying Osmond. James suggests that her early eagerness and vitality are essentially aimless. But in becoming the model for James's portrait, she seems to have surrendered some of her free creative impulse and vibrant sense of life.

The 'outside' observer in this scene is not the manly Lord Warburton, but the somewhat effete Ned Rosier. The scene opens with the aptly named Rosier's 'tilt' with Osmond, in which the *objet d'art* in question is explicitly Pansy, but also implicitly Isabel herself:

> 'No, I'm not thinking of parting with anything at all, Mr Rosier', said Osmond, with his eyes still on the eyes of his visitor.
>
> 'Ah, you want to keep, but not to add', Rosier remarked brightly.
>
> 'Exactly, I've nothing I wish to match.'   (p. 303)

Osmond's 'aestheticism' is a matter of acquisitiveness, of pride in property acquired, and is far removed from any pure creative or critical drive. Ned recognises that not only is Isabel now an impressive lady, but also that she is no mere 'collector's piece'. Unlike Osmond, he admires her for values beyond her 'decorative character', 'which his devotion to brittle wares had still not disqualified him to recognise' (p. 303).

It should be emphasised that the second portrait of Isabel is different in degree, not in kind, from the first. This much remains of natural setting in her own apartment where she has exercised her creativity: it is 'a large apartment with a concave ceiling', thus presenting, like the house in Albany, considerable opportunities for imaginative expansion. There are, moreover, always present 'an odour of flowers' and a 'subdued, diffused brightness', which suggest her influence – as interior decorator, if not as architect. Through the natural imagery he uses to describe her, James heightens our sense that she is more than artifact: 'the flower of her youth had not faded, it only hung more quietly on its stem' (p. 303).

If her field of action has diminished in size and scope, her relative importance in it seems subtly to have increased. Isabel has 'more the air of being able to wait' than that of surrender. Early in the novel, Isabel remains blissfully impervious when Ralph and Daniel Touchett playfully tease her. Now, in keeping with her passive but very real resistance, Isabel has developed the weapon of wit: 'Her humour had lately turned a good deal to sarcasm', James comments (p. 337). When Ned urges her to act as intermediary for him with

Osmond, he offers generously never to speak of her husband again 'save as an angel'. Isabel's reply is 'inscrutably' sardonic: 'The inducement's great' (p. 310). A little later she succinctly defines Osmond's character to Lord Warburton: 'He has a genius for upholstery' (p. 318). The tone is not unlike that of Madame Merle who compliments Osmond: 'Your rooms at least are perfect' (p. 205). Osmond, on the other hand, is completely humourless; James implies that both the moral sense and wit are inherent in any true apprehension of the Beautiful. When her husband fails to see the unconscious humour in Henrietta Stackpole's articles, Isabel 'even wondered if his sense of fun, or of the funny – which would be his sense of humour, wouldn't it? – were by chance defective' (p. 321).

Isabel Archer : Model or Artist?

Both Isabel herself and the other principal characters develop the habit of standing off and looking in a detached manner at her life as if it were a work of art at which they are spectators. Dorothea, we remember, was constantly being compared to works of art, whereas she longs to act and create. As Ralph says to Isabel, 'I content myself with watching you – with the deepest interest':

> She gave rather a conscious sigh. 'I wish I could be as interesting to myself as I am to you!'
> 'There you're not candid again; you're extremely interesting to yourself.'   (p. 131)

This self-consciousness, or concern with her own 'image', is one of Isabel's more peculiarly 'American' traits. The reader receives the distinct impression that Ralph is right, that Isabel enjoys playing the central role from the moment of her dramatic entrance at Garden-court. What she dislikes is the fact that she is not allowed herself to *write* the play, but only to perform in it – or, if you will, to sit, in apparent passivity, for her portrait.

Isabel's relation to artistic creativity, however, is destined to remain as conditional as Dorothea Brooke's. Many readers share her aunt Mrs Varian's belief in Isabel's potential creativity and are convinced that she participates to a great degree in James's fineness of perception and imaginative vision. Isabel is an artist figure, but her artistry never assumes a specific shape or form. As Mrs Touchett says of the description given by Isabel's sister, 'She spoke of her as you might speak of some young person of genius; but in that case I've not yet learned her special line' (p. 47). James has created a heroine endowed with power of observation, curiosity, delicacy of perception and comprehensiveness of vision. She none the less lacks the acute sense of control, form and discipline which are requisite to artistic expression. James comments of Mrs Varian's rumour: 'the girl had never attempted to write a book and had no desire for the laurels of authorship. She had no talent for expression and too little of the consciousness of genius' (pp. 52–3).

Isabel's only 'creative' act is alternately described as the painting of a self-portrait, and the erecting of a complicated architecture of consciousness. In fact, Isabel cannot paint a self-portrait; she can merely project an essentially static image of herself for others, serve as model for other 'artists' who manipulate her life. James's architectural metaphor, despite the title of the novel, is more pervasive and complex than the analogy of portraiture. It takes over from the latter probably because it more directly involves the heroine's own activity and spiritual effort. It remains to be seen why Isabel's architecture of consciousness, though more success- ful than the self-portrait, receives no concrete artistic embodiment.

A Transcendental Provincial Heroine

Many of James's reasons for making extensive use of architectural imagery are obvious. In the Preface, written many years after the novel, he lucidly disengages his intention of creating a 'House of Fiction' from the architecture of consciousness of the various characters, and from the series of fictional houses he presents in the work. If Isabel builds her own limited 'house of fiction', James in turn builds up around his young lady standing there 'in perfect isolation' a rather more complex architectural form.

Architecture, like the Jamesian novel of manners, is a pre-emi- nently social art. James's strong sense of aesthetic structure, moreover, finds its fitting embodiment in architecture. He seems indebted to Ralph Waldo Emerson's organic theory of art in which the latter describes a poem (or any literary work, for that matter) as having 'an architecture of its own', derived from the inmost heart of the work, the thought of its creator.[23] According to Thoreau as well, a literal house should be built from within outwards; he stresses the need for functionalism, for the house to express the character of its tenant.

There are indications that Isabel, like James, has imbibed aspects of the Transcendental aesthetic. At the time of Isabel's girlhood (as of James's young manhood), Albany would have been more or less directly under the influence of the New England tradition, a fact which James underlines by making the Touchetts Vermonters from just across the border. There is a certain oblique veracity in Osmond's remark that Isabel's 'sentiments were worthy of a radical newspaper or a Unitarian preacher' (p. 355). James remarks amusedly of Osmond's belief that 'she had no tradition and the moral horizon of a Unitarian minister' – 'Poor Isabel, who had never been able to understand Unitarianism!' (p. 355). He nevertheless makes it clear that she carries among her intellectual baggage, whether consciously or unconsciously, a New England tradition that began in puritanical soul-searching, and continued through Unitarian private worship and emphasis on reason and individualism to Transcendentalism.[24] From a self-reliant religion to a self-reliant philosophy was a very short step – one which Emerson, among others, took.

Furthermore, James demonstrates vividly Isabel's repugnance at several ideas and ambitions of her husband which 'she could never take in': 'To begin with, they were hideously unclean. She was not a daughter of the Puritans, but for all that she believed in such a thing as chastity and even as decency. It would appear that Osmond was far from doing anything of the sort; some of his traditions made her push back her skirts' (p. 356).[25] Although Isabel denies that she is a daughter of the Puritans, her moral integrity is a product of a long-standing characteristically American ethic.[26]

Isabel's innocence and inexperience, conditioned by her early reading and isolation in Albany, predispose her to a large, free, fluid vision of the human potential. But they also inhibit her from recognising the existence of evil in the world – for her the 'cup of experience' is 'a poisoned drink'. Ralph admonishes her, 'You want to see, but not to feel' (p. 132).[27] There are corners of the 'architecture of consciousness' which she is afraid to explore: 'With all her love of knowledge she had a natural shrinking from raising curtains and looking into unlighted corners. The love of knowledge coexisted in her mind with the finest capacity for ignorance' (p. 171). Her final decision to marry Osmond is foreshadowed as

an abyss into which she will plunge, immersing herself in
knowledge of his evil:

> Her imagination ... now hung back; there was a last vague space it
> couldn't cross – a dusky, uncertain tract which looked ambiguous
> and even slightly treacherous, like a moorland seen in the winter
> twilight. But she was to cross it yet.   (p. 260)

It is, in fact, the 'dusky, pestiferous tract' she had mentally
contrasted to her own garden of introspection.

Although her 'New Englandliness' is but feebly apprehended by
Isabel herself, James's criticisms of his heroine's vision are
consonant with his analysis of the failing of Emersonian Transcendentalism. He once wrote an essay claiming that Emerson's
determined innocence, optimism and failure to perceive evil in the
world were the besetting faults of the American mentality. He
deprecates Emerson's aesthetic blindness as well as his blindness to
evil. After visiting the Louvre and the Vatican with Emerson, he
claimed that there were chords in the older man – namely the
aesthetic – that just did not vibrate at all. For James, artistic integrity
embraces awareness of evil as well as optimism, a sense of form as
well as the moral sense. James's occasional ambivalence towards his
heroine can be traced, at least in part, to his attraction–repulsion for
Transcendentalism.[28]

Woman in Search of an Art

Isabel is not only a would-be Transcendental artist, however; she is
a would-be *woman* artist. Her womanhood, like her Transcendental
provincialism, is both incentive and deterrent to her ambitions.
There is little evidence that James takes seriously such creative
outlets for women as Jane Austen and George Eliot found. His only
literary woman in the novel is Henrietta Stackpole, and his portrait
of her is gently satirical. Moreover, even Henrietta can further her
exploration of English society only through marriage to one of its
members, the egregious Mr Bantling.[29] Henrietta's journalistic
instincts are drawn by the Countess Gemini's elucidation of 'the
position of woman in this city' (p. 370). For all her independence,
Henrietta herself begins finally to deplore the position of women in
general. When Caspar asks if Isabel is in need of help, Henrietta
replies, 'Most women always are' (p. 377).

Isabel, like the other three provincial heroines, discovers that the house is an ambiguous symbol: both her only potentially creative outlet, and the visible embodiment of 'the prison of womanhood'. Emma Woodhouse, eager for long, vigorous walks in the country, is confined for the most part to Hartfield, the nucleus of Mr Woodhouse's 'family circle', by his ill health, as Emma Bovary is constantly exclaiming, 'J'étouffe!' Her entrapment is very close to that of Dorothea with Casaubon or Isabel with Osmond. Flaubert, Eliot and James depict feelingly the horrors of sharing one's life with a person one despises.

At Gardencourt, as in Albany, Isabel has unlimited faith that she will escape any domestic prison such as that our earlier heroines found in Hartfield, Yonville and Lowick. The battle-lines are drawn in Isabel's early verbal skirmish with Madame Merle, when the two discuss the inevitable arrival of a young man with a moustache. Madame Merle indicates that his house would reveal to her his suitability or lack of suitability. Isabel protests, 'I don't care anything about his house', to which Madame Merle replies, 'That's very crude of you. When you've lived as long as I you'll see that every human being has his shell and that you must take the shell into account. By the shell I mean the whole envelope of circumstances' (p. 172). Furthermore, she adds, it is through one's possessions that one achieves self-expression: 'One's self – for other people – is one's expression of one's self; and one's house, one's furniture, one's garments, the books one reads, the company one keeps – these things are all expressive' (p. 173).

Madame Merle, rather than Isabel, seems at this point to be echoing the Jamesian view of the exigencies of form, since James himself is concerned with 'the whole envelope of circumstances', with what he calls elsewhere 'the very atmosphere of the mind'. But there is a serious discrepancy between the brilliance of Madame Merle's theory – which does embody a central psychological truth of the novel that Isabel is to learn only slowly and painfully – and her actual practice. The entire dialogue is a notably subtle instance of Jamesian irony – and irony with a double twist. On one level, James is underscoring Isabel's innocence pushed to the point of ignorance, in contrast with Madame Merle's experience and wisdom. On another level, however, James's double-edged irony comes into play when we apply Madame Merle's theory to Madame Merle. Her 'house', 'furniture', 'garments', 'books', the 'company' she keeps, do indeed express herself, and that self, it is suggested, is petty and calculating. Her interest is in the concrete possessions as status symbols, rather than as aesthetic values.

James in this scene brings to a focus the dichotomy between Isabel's Transcendental idealism and Madame Merle's opportunistic materialism as outlets for women. When the two define their personalities succinctly by reference to the material shell, James's sympathies are with the misguided innocence of his heroine, who retorts to Madame Merle, 'I don't know whether I succeed in expressing myself, but I know that nothing else expresses me. Nothing that belongs to me is any measure of me; everything's on the contrary a limit, a barrier; and a perfectly arbitrary one' (p. 173). At this point, Isabel, like Melville's Ahab, is determined to 'strike through the mask' of materialism, even while she resists a psychological truth. Her untutored 'Transcendental longings' are directed towards an immediate apprehension of the ideal; she is impatient of 'illusory' barriers or limits of self-expression.

Isabel comes to realise in the course of her European education the truth of Madame Merle's words, that a house can be a form of self-expression, not necessarily a barrier to it. She surpasses her mentor, however, in making the distinction between expressiveness and acquisitiveness. As Emerson emphasises, the power of the mind is that of fluxing external reality, of making the universe flow before it. Isabel's naïveté in this dialogue is underlined by her attitude towards clothing. In a statement reminiscent of Thomas Carlyle's *Sartor Resartus*, she claims, 'My clothes may express the dressmaker, but they don't express me. To begin with it's not my own choice that I wear them; they're imposed upon me by society' (p. 173).[30] She thus leaves herself open to attack in the form of a joke in bad taste from Madame Merle: ' "Should you prefer to go without them?" Madame Merle enquired in a tone which virtually terminated the discussion' (p. 173).[31]

THE LESSON OF EUROPE

As Isabel moves into a fallen world, she increasingly explores the interiors of houses and the interiors of the minds of others. From Transcendental self-reliance she moves to the assumption of responsibility for others, screening the real nature of her marriage from Ralph, supporting Pansy as well as she can. She learns to read the character of the tenant in the series of houses she visits or inhabits and thereby fulfils the quest for her own identity. In so doing she approaches, not Madame Merle's position, but that of the Jamesian artist.

From Gardencourt to the Roccanera: Isabel's Shaping Experiences

While still living at Gardencourt, and despite her protests that she will not judge a suitor by his house, she proceeds to do exactly that at Lockleigh, Lord Warburton's seat. She sees it as a well-appointed, comfortable prison house, surrounded by a moat. Warburton is an enlightened nobleman, but only up to a point. As Daniel Touchett comments, 'He seems to want to do away with a good many things, but he seems to want to remain himself. I suppose that's natural, but it's rather inconsistent' (p. 70). James, in naming the house, may be thinking of Tennyson's 'Locksley Hall', with its warning of imminent revolution: 'Slowly comes a hungry people, as a lion, creeping nigher / Glares at one that nods and winks behind a slowly-dying fire.'[32] In any case, Lockleigh is literally 'locked up' for the Misses Molyneux, Warburton's sisters.

Although Warburton is probably the most charming man in the novel, one finds it difficult to conceive of Isabel's ever accepting a status similar to that of the Misses Molyneux.[33] They follow the Miltonic dictum, 'He for God only, and she for God in him.' They are ornamental, with eyes 'like balanced basins ... set in parterres, among the geraniums' (p. 72), and James comments, 'if they had a fault it was a want of play of mind' (p. 73). Isabel exercises her wit on this passivity, in which 'liberalism' is merely an easy convention where the English nobility have always had room to move about.

Although Warburton's appeal is romantic, Isabel feels that 'a territorial, a political, a social magnate had conceived the design of drawing her into the system in which he rather invidiously lived and moved.' The words 'social, territorial, political' emphasise his mere worldliness, whereas her aspirations are Transcendental; 'virtually she had a system and an orbit of her own' (p. 94). Warburton facetiously specifies the materials on which her imagination seeks to work: 'You select great materials: the foibles, the affliction of human nature, the peculiarities of nations' (p. 77). What he defines is, in fact, the province of the international novelist whom Isabel resembles.

Mrs Touchett's house in Florence, the Crescentini, is redolent with sinister and historic atmosphere and represents Isabel's initiation to the Continent: 'To live in such a place was, for Isabel, to hold to her ear all day a shell of the sea of the past' (p. 208). Ironically, Mrs Touchett herself lacks the romantic imagination to appreciate her house. She is like the romantic Isabel, however, in exalting her independence. She lives according to a 'masculine' code, and Ralph indicates that she is more 'gubernatorial' than his father (p. 42). What is independence in Isabel has hardened into rigidity in her aunt. As Daniel Touchett thinks, Isabel 'reminded him of his wife when his wife was in her teens' (p. 57). Isabel is saved from this hardness by the fact that 'she carried within herself a great fund of life' (p. 41).

Isabel falls as much in love with Gilbert Osmond's houseful of romantic objects as with the man himself. His house in Florence, like Osmond himself, has that 'air of undervalued merit which in Italy ... always gracefully invests any one who confidently assumes a perfectly passive attitude.' Just as this passivity is mere pretence on Osmond's part, so the house takes on the character of a 'mask': 'It had heavy lids, but no eyes' (p. 192). It is closed to fresh perceptions, and at the same time it frustrates intelligent curiosity on the part of others. Osmond's garden is narrow and limited, 'productive chiefly of tangles of wild roses', just as Osmond's natural instincts have become warped and stultified.[34]

The last major dwelling in *Portrait*, Osmond's Roman palace, the Roccanera, is even more prison-like than the Florentine villa. Here not only the docile Pansy, but the vibrant Isabel, is immured. Ned Rosier looks on the Roccanera as a 'dungeon' rather than a palace, 'a kind of domestic fortress, a pile which bore a stern old Roman name, which smelt of historic deeds, of crime and craft and violence' (p. 301). It has no garden, but only an unhealthy 'damp court' (p. 301). Translated literally the 'stern old Roman name' the Palace bears signifies 'the black rock', to which Isabel has moved from 'Garden-court'. The loss of Isabel's child in the first year of marriage reminds us of the barrenness of this union symbolised by the house.

Madame Merle and Osmond, who are jointly responsible for incarcerating Isabel in the Roccanera, themselves show little sense of architecture. Rather, they are collectors of miniatures, of bric-à-brac. As the Countess Gemini remarks, Madame Merle has never succeeded in finding a home of her own and lives parasitically, 'getting to know every one and staying with them free of expense' (p. 446). She has aspired to marry Caesar, but in reality has only had an affair with Osmond. Her fitting emblem, as she herself wryly recognises, is a cracked and mended cup (p. 166), and we remember that Will Ladislaw saw Rosamond Lydgate as a crystal he would like to crack. Madame Merle talks like 'a volume of smooth twaddle' (p. 57) and when discussing art remembers the minor details, not the total effect. Ralph describes her accurately as 'the great round world itself'. Ironically, if Isabel chooses Madame Merle as her initial model for an ideal lady, Pansy Osmond prefers Isabel, not knowing that Madame Merle, whom she rather dislikes, is her own mother.

Similarly, Osmond's human values are reduced to the single criterion of taste. He is indeed 'provincial', as he claims to be at one point, but scarcely 'sweetly' so. He tries to reduce his daughter to a set of pictures (p. 434) and his wife to 'handled ivory' (p. 254) or a 'silver plate' reflecting his own image (p. 29). Finally, Isabel realises she has become not even an aesthetic object, but 'an applied hung-up tool, as senseless and convenient as mere shaped wood and iron' (p. 451). Osmond lives in 'a sorted, sifted, arranged world' (p. 73). As Isabel remarks mockingly, 'that's a very pleasant life ... to renounce everything but Corregio!' (p. 223). One is reminded of Dorothea's scorn for the 'Corregiosities' in her uncle's drawing-room after she has come from the squalor of the village. It is characteristic of Osmond that he should resent feeling an 'atom' in 'that greatest of human temples', St Peter's, where Isabel's imagination has space to soar (pp. 246–7).

If James criticised the Transcendentalists for lacking a sense of form, as well as a sense of evil, the development of these two senses constitutes the lesson of Europe for Henry James, and for Isabel Archer as well. To that degree, Isabel needs to be schooled by the Europeanised Americans Osmond and Merle. There is a distinct possibility, in fact, that the keenly appreciative, but calculating and manipulative co-conspirators are modelled on the sinister ex-lovers and seducers, Madame de Merteuil and the Vicomte de Valmont, in Choderlos de Laclos's eighteenth-century French novel, *Les Liaisons dangereuses.*[35]

Henrietta Stackpole and Caspar Goodwood, the itinerant Americans, function as foils to the two Europeanised Americans. If Osmond and Merle lack a moral sense, Goodwood and Stackpole lack a sense of the past, of aesthetics. They are the active, bustling Americans not really open to the European experience, and Isabel is

caught in the middle between them and the Europeanised conspir-
ators. The dwelling-place associated with Henrietta is a steamship,
suggested by the 'stack' in her last name, or, as James remarks at
one point, a railway station (p. 398). She has formed all of her
impressions of Europe in advance.

Caspar's last name may suggest the good, solid building
materials of the conventional American marriage Isabel rejects.
Osmond, in fact, compares him to a tall tower. Like Henrietta, he
is somehow rigid and unyielding. Apparently to emphasise
Isabel's finally 'freeing' herself from the passion of Caspar, James
expanded the text of the New York Edition from the original, 'His
kiss was like a flash of lightning; when it was dark again she was
free', to a complex passage underlining Caspar's threatening
virility (p. 482). James probably had in mind the similar scene in
Middlemarch, which, however, has the opposite effect on the
ardent Dorothea. Towards the end of the novel, Dorothea, looking
out of the study window at Lowick, is startled by a flash of
lightning, turns abruptly and falls into Will's arms, having finally
exorcised the ghost of Casaubon. It may be that, as Leon Edel
thinks, Isabel is afraid, both physically and emotionally, of 'this act
of possession'.[36] Perhaps, even, it does not fit her concept of 'a
lady'. On the other hand, James may be in full sympathy with
Isabel's refutation of Caspar's 'hard manhood'. She may want to
live in a 'house', or private world, of her own creation, rather than
in one of Caspar's, however substantial and secure it may be. As
Dorothea Krook points out, 'James shared his heroine's fear of,
and even revulsion from, the sexual passion in its more violent,
importunate forms, and for reasons *mutatis mutandis* essentially
similar to hers ... as a threat to the two things, one "public" and
other "private" or personal, that were most precious to him – his
ideal of civilization on the one side, his aspiration to dedicate his
life to the practice of his art on the other.'[37] Isabel, moreover, is
determined to remain a free agent. With her puritanical outlook,
she may fear enslavement to Caspar's passion, which might make
of her a chattel wife. Freedom implies the containment and control
of passion requisite to civilised life.

Edel is astute in his observation that one need not apologise for
an Isabel Archer when mentioning her in the same breath as great
heroines of passion like Emma Bovary and Anna Karenina. James
is unique in having created a heroine imbued with much of his
own coolness and detachment.[38]

By the end of the novel, Isabel finally mediates the positions of, at the one extreme, the honest but unadaptable Stackpole and Goodwood and, at the other, the sinister Merle and Osmond. Her choice of Europe is essentially James's own, even while she and her creator remain intrinsically American in their moral fibre and intensity.[39]

Isabel's Architecture of Consciousness

Not only James himself, but the characters, use architectural metaphors drawn from their literal houses to describe each other. Osmond speaks truth in jest in addressing Isabel: 'I myself am as rusty as a key that has no lock to fit it. It polished me up a little to talk with you – not that I venture to pretend I can turn that very complicated lock I suspect your intellect of being!' (p. 217).[40]

Most revealingly, architectural imagery is used by the two finest sensibilities in the novel, Isabel herself and Ralph Touchett. Ralph immediately senses the extreme complexity of Isabel's architecture of consciousness: 'He surveyed the edifice from the outside and admired it greatly. ... But he felt that he saw it only by glimpses and that he had not yet stood under the roof' (p. 63). Isabel, by the same token, wants to enter Ralph's 'private apartments' and see what is going on within, since she realises it is not the 'dancing' and gaiety he pretends (p. 61).

Throughout the novel James progressively transfers his own metaphorical rendering of reality to his heroine's mind. The transference reaches a climax in the fireside vigil scene which James sees as the finest in the novel, and which is so close in effect and in imagery to Dorothea's tearful vigil in *Middlemarch*. Isabel's recognition of Madame Merle's and Osmond's intimacy has been precipitated by her surprising them in conversation, Madame Merle standing while the usually punctilious Osmond remains seated. In the analogous scene in *Middlemarch*, Dorothea descends unexpectedly on her admirer, Will, in a seemingly compromising situation with Rosamond Lydgate. Suspecting Madame Merle's collusion, Isabel has found herself led 'into the mansion of his own [Osmond's] habitation', and she now recognises that:

It was the house of darkness, the house of dumbness, the house of suffocation. Osmond's beautiful mind gave it neither light nor air; Osmond's beautiful mind indeed seemed to peep down from a small high window and mock at her.   (p. 353)

To Osmond's dismay, however, he finds that he is himself locked within a larger, finer intelligence than his own, because she judges him. She has kept a part of herself from him before marriage, and now he finds himself 'with the door closed behind, as it were – set down face to face with it' (p. 352).[41]

When Isabel tells Osmond that she must return to Gardencourt because Ralph is dying, she bursts through the door of his study without knocking (p. 436). We recollect her old objection, to Madame Merle, that houses are but physical limits and barriers to her and sense something of her former Transcendental fire. Now, however, her motive is not romantic idealism, but rather deep feeling, love and compassion for Ralph. By this point she has so transcended her early egotism that she has been able to feel pity even for Serena Merle.

She performs the journey to England 'with sightless eyes', no longer because she lives in a romantically conditioned garden of introspection, but because she is rendering the meanings of a painfully real experience in architectural terms:

> Now that she was in the secret, now that she knew something that so much concerned her the eclipse of which had made life resemble an attempt to play whist with an imperfect pack of cards, the truth of things, their mutual relations, their meaning, and for the most part their horror, rose before her with a kind of architectural vastness.   (p. 457)

This inner vision based on suffering, her acceptance of limits, death, tragedy, permits her finally to see the ghost at Gardencourt. After Ralph's death, she once again sees herself in active relation to external life: 'There were tears in Isabel's eyes, but they were not tears that blinded' (p. 473). But after Caspar's 'act of possession', 'she had moved through the darkness (for she saw nothing) and reached the door. ... She had not known where to turn; but she knew now. There was a very straight path' (p. 482). In fleeing Caspar, she is fleeing a passion that blinds her to her surroundings. She has learned to take into account 'the whole envelope of circumstances', and the American's single-mindedness would exclude too much. If, after Ralph's death, the inner architecture dominates the outer, it does so with certain knowledge based on painful experience, not on Transcendental romantic preconceptions. And Isabel is indeed close to the perceptions of the realistic psychological novelist who created her.

Every reader of *The Portrait* has his own theory as to why Isabel returns to Osmond in Rome after rebelling for long enough to hasten to Ralph's deathbed at Gardencourt. Whatever the reasons that can be educed for Isabel's return – existential commitment, flight from Caspar Goodwood, fidelity to the marriage bond, the protection of Pansy, the belief that Isabel, like Strether in *The Ambassadors*, must gain nothing for herself – it remains evident that she is spiritually free and launched on a life of fine perception. What is not so often remarked is that she chooses, of her own free will, to remain in the visibly fallen world of continental Europe, while it is Madame Merle who must return to America – perhaps for a refresher course in innocence!

Nevertheless, there remains an ambiguity at the end of the novel, and that is neither Isabel's fear of Caspar's manhood nor James's own sexual ambivalences. It is, rather, that James has created a heroine capable of constructing a complex architecture of consciousness, melding the two different cultures she has experienced, but he has denied her the power of expression. If Isabel, like Strether, has overcome her early Transcendental blindness to evil, should she not also have overcome the blindness to form? We are left uneasy not so much at the fact that Isabel renounces, but that she renounces in favour of nothing in particular. Strether has his art, Maggie Verver has her Prince. Perhaps Maggie proves, in fact, that the Isabel-figure continues to haunt James throughout his career to the point that he has to come back to it much as William Faulkner was to come back to the figure of Quentin Compson in *Absalom, Absalom!* Perhaps the final abyss James's imagination could not cross was that of feminine creativity. He has painted a subtle, moving Portrait of a Lady, but has stopped short of a Portrait of a Lady as Artist. It is true that Austen and Eliot, our women novelists, also stop short of such a portrait, but I have tried to suggest that they are simply recognising democratically that the majority of potentially creative women will never have their own unique opportunities.

Whatever our uncertainties at the ending – James himself admits that 'The *whole* of anything is never told; you can only take what groups together' – he and his heroine have shaped a spacious architecture which, by its openness, invites us to speculate beyond the given. It is fitting that the novel concludes, not with the heroine regarded as portrait or object, but an enigmatical and complex architect of her own fate.

Epilogue

Henry James said of *Middlemarch*, 'If we write novels so, how shall we write History?'[1] He felt the work 'sets a limit ... to the development of the old-fashioned English novel'.[2] D. H. Lawrence was later to disagree, claiming that Eliot had already broken through the limits, that it was she 'who started it all. ... It was she who started putting all the action inside'.[3]

All four of our authors enlarged the scope of the novel by focussing on a feminine consciousness and giving birth to the psychological novel as we know it today. In the case of Austen and Eliot, the author's consciousness, as well as the heroine's, is feminine. But it could be argued that Flaubert and James equally share a 'feminine' sensibility, as their (and perhaps our) age defined it – sensitivity, emotional responsiveness, inwardness – just as Austen and Eliot share a 'masculine' one – detachment, objectivity, wit, intellect, as well as a strong historical sense and a tendency to social analysis. Not only Jane Austen, but also Flaubert, wrote finely chiselled miniatures. George Eliot, more so than Henry James, wrote ambitious panoramas. Stereotypes about 'masculine' and 'feminine' creative sensibilities simply do not apply, or apply only when we admit the possibility of crossovers by the imagination of the artist.

It is perhaps appropriate that our four provincial heroines – those 'frail vessels of the affections' – should provide the focal points for four highly experimental novels. Jane Austen first conceived the notion of dispensing with plot and creating a heroine so vital, irrepressible and imaginative that the entire novel comprises the dialectic of her limited point of view and Austen's discreet, subtle corrections. Flaubert, too, uses a heroine – or anti-heroine – as a vehicle for the indictment of nineteenth–century France and its cancerous bourgeois mediocrity. His skill is all the more impressive in that he succeeds in arousing the reader's indignation despite the fact that his heroine–victim is herself incapable of any tragic recognition. For Eliot and James, on the other hand, the *donnée* is a heroine who comes close to attaining the comprehensive vision of her creator.

As we have seen, some critics would like to see Isabel Archer (or Maggie Verver in *The Golden Bowl*) as a Jamesian artist, but it is impossible to advance this claim without blurring the distinction between art and life. For years critics and readers have recognised the close affinities between James's heroines and himself, yet it is the female protagonists, rather than the male, who most frequently lack any power of articulation.

Blurring the distinction between art and life, between wish and reality, is a temptation we all face with these novels. One can sympathise with the critic who sees in Dorothea Brooke a kind of 'talisman' for young women'[4] or with students who feel ultimately frustrated that positive role models such as Emma, Dorothea and Isabel do not achieve more. Instead of condemning such simplistic or reductive critiques, it might help to recognise that the four authors as well all had to confront, in one form or another, the fate of the creative drive in a hostile or indifferent society. All four circumscribe woman's destiny in society's. Their new vision of character and destiny demanded that the novelist 'break the mould' of the traditional form, as James put it. In a variation on the Pygmalion and Galatea motif, James – recognising the actual and potential importance of the 'frail vessels of the affections' for the art of fiction – first fell in love with Eliot's Dorothea and then with his own creation, Isabel. But James's Galatea is not without the ambition to be herself a creator.

Virginia Woolf claimed that a woman writer needed an independent income and 'a room of her own'. It is not surprising that interiors of houses, and architectural imagery generally, loom large in all four of these novels. Both Eliot and James view the novel itself as an architectural form, even as their heroines seek to transform 'the prison of womanhood' into a spacious edifice, created by themselves, in which their imaginations will have room to soar. In a literary tradition dominated by men, the relatively young genre of fiction afforded fertile ground for experimentation by women writers, and by male writers concerned with the reordering of society which must start with its nucleus, male–female relations.

It is tempting to imagine our four heroines (as Woolf imagined women writers) together in 'a room of their own' speculating on the role of women today. To what extent, they might ask, have women succeeded in 'widening the skirts of light'? That one is tempted to create such an imaginary dialogue supports my view that we care about these heroines as if we had known them in life. The novels in which they appear deserve a critical methodology applied to them that does not simply trace feminist themes, but gives full justice to the dynamism of the text. This dynamism first captivated Henry

James, and has inspired the fictional and real-life heroines of the twentieth century, striving for their own independence. It will continue to furnish our imaginations for centuries to come.

Emma Woodhouse is the forerunner of Virginia Woolf's Mrs Graham *(To the Lighthouse)* and Willa Cather's Myra Henshawe *(My Mortal Enemy)*, both bungling matchmakers for want of an authentic art. Flaubert's Emma Bovary is recognisable not only in Carol Kennicott, that 'Madame Bovary of the western plains', but also in Betty Friedan's alcoholic or Valium-addicted housewives of the Eastern suburbs. Dorothea Brooke might have been a Civil Rights activist or anti-war protester in the 1960s, and would have campaigned for the Equal Rights Amendment in the 1970s and 1980s, as a twentieth-century George Eliot would have been close to Jean-Paul Sartre's position that one should not write novels as long as there is a child starving in the world. And what of Isabel Archer? In the twentieth century, she might have written her own novel.

Notes

Notes to Chapter 1: 'Emma's Daughters'

1. Henry James, *The Portrait of a Lady* (Boston, Mass.: Houghton Mifflin Riverside Edition, 1956) p. 54. Hereafter the novel will be designated *Portrait* and cited in the text.

2. There is, of course, a long-standing tradition of creative provincial heroes as well. One thinks, for instance, of Balzac's Lucien de Rubempré, Stendhal's Julien Sorel and Hardy's Jude Fawley. French novelists, in particular, have always been intensely aware of the literary possibilities inherent in the theme of provincial entrapment and in its correlative, the theme of the corruption encountered by an ambitious provincial transplanted to Paris. Our very point, however, in focussing on these four women is that we *can* think of them in almost the same terms as of a Julien Sorel or of a Lord Jim. They are ambitious and idealistic in ways that had hitherto been reserved to male characters, and they mark a distinct break from the literary tradition of feminine helplessness or of merely moral supportiveness. The assumption of a freedom bordering on the masculine privileges is evident in Emma Woodhouse's efforts to treat men as equals rather than as superiors, in Dorothea Brooke's desire to shape humanitarian reforms, and in Isabel Archer's scorn for chaperonage and in her desire to sit up late with the men. It is important to remember, too, that provincial isolation weighed even more heavily upon women than upon men, as their movements were more narrowly circumscribed, their outlets fewer.

3. Emily Dickinson, *Complete Poems*, ed. Thomas H. Johnson (Boston, Mass.: Little, Brown, 1960) pp. 263–4.

4. R. P. Utter and G. B. Needham, *Pamela's Daughters* (New York, 1936).

5. Ian Watt, *The Rise of the Novel* (Berkeley, Cal., 1959) p. 161.

6. Jane Austen, *Emma* (Boston, Mass.: Houghton Mifflin Riverside Edition, 1957) p. 47.

7. George Eliot, *Middlemarch* (Boston, Mass.: Houghton Mifflin Riverside Edition, 1956) p. 161. Hereafter the novel will be cited in the text.

8. Alexander Welsh, 'George Eliot and the Romance', *Nineteenth Century Fiction*, 14 (1959–60) 241–54.

9. Gustave Flaubert, *Madame Bovary* (Paris: Editions Garnier, 1960) p. 83.

10. Henry James, 'Gustave Flaubert', in *The Future of the Novel*, ed. Leon Edel (New York: Vintage Books, 1956) p. 138.

11. Harry Levin, *The Gates of Horn: A Study of Five French Realists* (New York, 1963) p. 247.

12. Ibid., p. 248.

13. Charlotte Ramsey Lennox, *The Female Quixote: or, The Adventures of*

Arabella (London, 1810). Mary Lascelles, in *Jane Austen and Her Art* (London: Oxford University Press, 1963), points out that Mrs Lennox's novel was a major influence on Jane Austen (pp. 41–83).

14. Anthony Thorlby, *Gustave Flaubert and the Art of Realism* (New Haven, Conn.: Yale University Press, 1957) p. 35.

15. James, quoted in Appendix to *Portrait*, p. 483.

16. James, 'Preface' to *Portrait*, p. 7.

Notes to Chapter 2: Emma Woodhouse

1. Henry James, *The Portrait of a Lady* (Boston, Mass.: Houghton Mifflin Riverside Edition, 1956) p. 54.

2. Jane Austen, *Memoir*, p. 157; quoted in Mary Lascelles, *Jane Austen and Her Art* (London: Oxford University Press, 1963) p. 69. From the evidence of available criticism on *Emma*, Austen was prophetic about the reception of her heroine. If one adds to the critics hostile to Emma Woodhouse those who simply do not understand her, they easily outnumber such supporters and defenders as John Henry Newman. Of the 'enemies', the most acerbic and controversial is Marvin Mudrick who, in his *Jane Austen: Irony as Defense and Discovery* (Princeton, N.J.: Princeton University Press, 1952), argues that Emma fears commitment because of what the twentieth century refers to as a Lesbian tendency. He goes so far as to say of Harriet Smith, Emma's little protégée, that 'for a time at least, Emma is in love with her: a love unphysical and inadmissible, even perhaps undefinable in such a society, and therefore safe' (p. 203). Edmund Wilson rides the same Freudian hobby-horse in 'A Long Talk about Jane Austen', *Jane Austen: A Collection of Critical Essays*, ed. Ian Watt (Englewood Cliffs, N.J.: Prentice-Hall, 1963).

  The psychoanalytic readings of Emma's 'problem' – variously defined as frigidity, narcissism, immaturity and Lesbianism – are often supported or extended by attempts to offer the reader an alternative heroine, Harriet Smith or Jane Fairfax. Susan J. Morgan, in 'Emma Woodhouse and the Charms of Imagination', *Studies in the Novel*, VIII, 1 (Spring 1975), in effect rewrites the novel with Jane Fairfax as the centre, seeing the open ending as a function of Jane's departure and our unsatisfied curiosity about her (p. 48). She seems to forget that Jane Austen could have written a novel about a Jane Fairfax if she so desired. In fact, she did: it was entitled *Mansfield Park* or *Persuasion*, not *Emma*. Wayne C. Booth, in *The Rhetoric of Fiction* (Chicago, Ill.: University of Chicago Press, 1961), recognises Emma as the heroine, but reluctantly: 'Jane is superior to Emma in most respects except the stroke of good fortune that made Emma the heroine of the book' (p. 249). Marilyn Butler, in *Jane Austen and the War of Ideas* (Oxford: Oxford University Press, 1975), judiciously assigns Emma her place as 'the rightful heroine', but then feels impelled to launch a gratuitous attack on Jane Fairfax who, she claims, 'is almost as much an anti-heroine as Mary Crawford' (p. 269).

3.   In a useful summary of trends, traditional and recent, in Austen criticism, 'Jane Austen Studies: a Portrait of the Lady and her Critics', *Studies in the Novel*, VIII, 1 (Spring 1975), J. Donald Crowley comes back to F. R. Leavis's celebrated statement, 'Austen belongs in the "Great Tradition" because she makes tradition for those coming after her' (p. 152). Because she wrote no prefaces, no manifestoes on the art of fiction – only a few semi-facetious letters – it is all too easy to assume, with Henry James, that 'our dear, everybody's dear Jane' composed intuitively, in the intervals of dropped stitches in the parlour. In fact, particularly in *Northanger Abbey* and *Emma*, fiction itself is already becoming a self-reflective act, one which is to lead later in the nineteenth century to a Flaubert, a George Eliot, a Henry James. Not the least of her contributions to the art was to adapt the Don Quixote theme to a heroine, Emma Woodhouse, and thus begin a small but important tradition of imaginative heroines who are themselves would-be artists.

4.   When I delivered an earlier draft of this chapter, focussing on the portrait of Harriet (Stong College Jane Austen Symposium, York University, 26 February 1976), I had not had the benefit of reading two recent critics who deal with the portrait in somewhat similar terms: Joseph Wiesenfarth, in 'Austen and Apollo', *Jane Austen Today*, ed. Joel Weinsheimer (Athens, Georgia: University of Georgia Press, 1975), and Bruce Stovel, in 'Comic Symmetry in Jane Austen's *Emma*', *The Dalhousie Review*, 57, 3 (Autumn 1977). The portrait is not, however, central to either article. Wiesenfarth is primarily concerned with the Pygmalion–Galatea myth as applied to both Emma–Harriet and Mr Knightley–Emma. He does some fancy footwork to prove that Emma is unconsciously painting the elegant Jane, not Harriet, only to conclude, after this unnecessary step, that 'the more closely Harriet's portrait resembles the elegance of Jane Fairfax, the more closely it resembles Emma's own elegance' (p. 55). He sees the portrait as narcissistic, but shows no interest in Emma's artistic motivation. Stovel's main concern is with structural echoes in the novel, of which the portrait is merely one which happens to reflect what Emma does to Harriet in life: 'she transforms Harriet's actual self into a monstrous new identity fashioned in the image of Emma herself' (p. 454).

5.   Jane Austen, *Emma* (Boston, Mass.: Houghton Mifflin Riverside Edition, 1957) p. 1. All subsequent page references will appear in the text and imply this edition.

6.   References to water are used sparingly, but revealingly, to suggest all the worlds, emotional and intellectual as well as physical, which lie just beyond Emma's reach. It is ironic that Emma herself is the first to employ a water image in the novel, but in the conventional, non-experiential terms of the romances which Jane Austen parodies or satirises:

> There does seem to be a something in the air of Hartfield which gives love exactly the right direction, and sends it into the very channel where it ought to flow.

> > The course of true love
> > never did run smooth

> A Hartfield edition of Shakespeare would have a long note on that passage.   (p. 159)

Jane Austen's own references to the sea and to watering-places, in contrast to Emma's, are always real, not figurative.

7.   J. S. Clarke, Librarian to the Prince Regent, asked her to attempt either a book about an intellectual clergyman or an ambitious historical novel. Her response was, 'No, I must keep to my own style and go on in my own way; and though I may never succeed again in that, I am convinced that I should totally fail in any other' (letter to J. S. Clarke, 1 April 1816). To clinch the point, her 'Plan of a Novel, According to Hints from Various Quarters' is a parody fulfilment of the Revd J. S. Clarke's request. It is an 'anti-*Emma*' whose heroine is all sentiment, no wit. Jane Austen concludes her bizarre outline of this heroine's peregrinations and melodramatic adventures by shedding a great deal of light on her real purpose in *Emma*: 'The name of the work *not* to be *Emma* – but of the same sort as S and S. and P and P' (William Heath (ed.), *Discussions of Jane Austen* (Boston, Mass.: D. C. Heath, 1961) p. 6).

8.   Quoted by Lascelles, *Jane Austen and Art*, pp. 135–6; orig. publ. 1894 as Preface to *Pride and Prejudice*, p. xv.

9.   Ibid., pp. 197–8.

10.   Also quoted by Mark Schorer, 'The Humiliation of Emma Wood-house', in Watt (ed.), *Jane Austen: A Collection of Critical Essays*, p. 101. At the beginning Emma has no profound knowledge even of Highbury; she is permitted to associate only with the Bateses and Mrs Goddard. Austen refers to this social world as a restricted circle in which Mr Woodhouse is accustomed to dominate: 'he could command the visits of his own little circle, in a great measure as he liked' (p. 13).

11.   As Booth snorts, 'Emma at carpet-work! If she knows herself indeed' (*Rhetoric of Fiction*, p. 261). The reader is invited to imagine Emma in the role of that faithful Penelope, Lady Bertram in *Mansfield Park*, blissfully and lethargically occupied with her carpet-work and her pug. Austen ensures that we not only laugh at Emma, however, but also sympathise with her; Emma's assumption that 'declining life' leads to declining sensations is based on her observation of her father, not on a realistic assessment of her own future direction.

12.   By Miss Lascelles, in particular.

13.   Emma herself is well on the way to leading a nun-like existence with her father, but invites our compassion because she never sees it as self-sacrifice. We are told at one point that Emma has been reading

Madame de Genlis's *Adelaide and Theodore* (London, 1783), whose plot concerns a young girl named Cecilia who is forced by her father to enter a convent and take her vows, in order to separate her from a lover. She dies young. Madame de Genlis was herself a governess to the Duke of Chartres's children, and thus the reference seems relevant to both Jane's fate and Emma's. (See the plot summary in the footnote to Mary Wollstonecraft's reference to Madame de Genlis in *A Vindication of the Rights of Woman*, ed. Carol H. Poston (New York: Norton Critical Edition, 1975) p. 104.)

14.   Lionel Trilling, Introduction to *Emma* (Riverside Edition) p. xiii. By the Victorian period, Thomas Holbrook, in Mrs Gaskell's *Cranford* (1853), is a yeoman recently become property owner and a well-read man, if rather unpolished in manners. It is not beyond reason that he should aspire to the hand of Miss Matty, a clergyman's daughter, and indeed he would have succeeded had it not been for the incurable snobbishness of her elder sister.

15.   Miss Lascelles also points to the scene outside Ford's as evidence for Austen's identification with her heroine. She sees Highbury as complete in itself, as a microcosm 'where definition is so sharp and scale so exactly kept the contrasts which it offers within itself are sufficient' (*Jane Austen and Her Art*, p. 180). A number of critics have noted that Emma embodies certain aspects of Austen's own creativity. Barbara Hardy, in *A Reading of Jane Austen* (London: Peter Owen, 1975), sees an artistic pilgrimage as the common thread tying together Austen's novels. David Lee Minter, in 'Aesthetic Vision and the World of *Emma*', *Nineteenth Century Fiction*, xxi, 1 (June 1966), argues that the heroine attempts 'to force an aesthetic ideal upon her world', to make it 'as rich and vital and beautiful as she feels herself potentially to be' (p. 51). Occasionally, however, he seems to me to be too prone to excuse Emma's blunders on the basis of the mediocrity of her surroundings. He seems a bit hard on Miss Bates, for instance, in saying that she 'exhausts her wit' in her reply to Frank Churchill's proposal of the guessing game at Box Hill. After all, she shows a perfect humility and self-understanding totally lacking in Emma's thoughtless riposte. None of the critics, however, examines in any detail the relationships between Emma's overtly and covertly artistic acts, her feminist presentiments, and Austen's own attitudes towards both women writers and the representation of women in fiction.

16.   Despite the satirical tone, it is important to recognise that even here Austen reinforces our belief in Emma's potential, reminding us that she 'ought not to have failed of' 'the degree of excellence' which she would like to set for herself.

17.   The Bateses, on the other hand, she has been accustomed to treat as pasteboard figures. We see her managing her father's whims by getting him and John Knightley off the subject of watering-places. But to do this she slips in the Bateses as though they were inanimate objects: 'You seem to have forgotten Mrs and Miss Bates ... I have not heard one inquiry after them' (p. 78). The remark anticipates her

later, more dangerous, use of Frank and Harriet as mere objects in an artistic arrangement. Emma is so accustomed to treating Miss Bates as part of the furniture that she simply never listens to her. It is Emma who in a sense prevents us from viewing directly Jane Fairfax's epistolary style. She judges Jane from her aunt, and escapes the letters themselves whenever possible. Jane's letters are doubtless more cogent than Miss Bates's summaries of them. Indeed, Miss Bates suggests 'we will turn to her letter, and I am sure she tells her own story a great deal better than I can tell it for her' (p. 123). But Emma never gives herself the chance to find out, and departs in haste. Reginald Farrer even calls Miss Bates 'an essentially wise woman' ('On *Emma*', in Heath (ed.), *Discussions of Jane Austen*, p. 103).

18. Charlotte Ramsey Lennox's Arabella, in *The Female Quixote* (London, 1810), makes a similar error when she is almost seduced by her father's footman, thinking him a prince in disguise. Mrs Lennox was also satirising the romances on which her heroine has been raised, and Miss Lascelles points out that *The Female Quixote* was one of Jane Austen's favourite novels (*Jane Austen and Her Art*, p. 55).

19. The image of Miss Bates haunting the abbey awakens echoes of *Northanger Abbey* with its satire of the Gothic which she was also preparing for publication in 1816.

20. Robert A. Donovan, in 'The Mind of Jane Austen', in Weinsheimer (ed.), *Jane Austen Today*, signals resemblances between Emma's caustic wit at Box Hill and Austen's exercised at the expense of friends in her correspondence. The difference is that Austen's is purely private, whereas Emma's witticism exposes Miss Bates to public ridicule (p. 112).

21. See Minter, 'Aesthetic Vision', for example, and Booth, who admits that 'regulated hatred' is only part of Austen's world, but 'the hatred of viciousness is there, and there is enough vice in evidence to make Emma almost shine by comparison' (*Rhetoric of Fiction*, p. 263).

22. Joseph M. Duffy, Jr, affirms that Harriet enables Emma to live vicariously, experiencing a series of courtships of which she is herself afraid, even in a physical sense ('Emma: the Awakening from Innocence', *ELH*, xxi (March 1954) 40). Marilyn Butler approaches the novel from the perspective of social history rather than psychoanalysis, but comes to a similar conclusion: namely, that Emma is escaping the bounds of 'propriety' by matchmaking for Harriet as a substitute for herself (*Jane Austen and the War of Ideas*, p. 251). She realises that Austen satirises Harriet as 'a primitivist's heroine' (p. 267), but fails to perceive that the satirical eye is not just Austen's, but Emma's own. Mudrick affirms that Emma will continue her 'infatuations with women' even after marriage (*Jane Austen: Irony*, p. 206). Suffice it to say that the text affords little evidence in support of this thesis, and that the metaphors characterising Emma's realisation of her passion for Mr Knightley point in exactly the opposite direction.

23.   Mudrick, *Jane Austen: Irony*, p. 190.

24.   Although Emma is speaking here rashly and from total inexperience, the sensible Fanny Price makes a similar complaint: 'Let him have all the perfections in the world, I think it ought not to be set down as certain that a man must be acceptable to every woman he may happen to like himself' (*Mansfield Park* (New York: Modern Library, n.d.) p. 684).

25.   We may never know whether Jane Austen had read Mary Wollstonecraft's *Vindication of the Rights of Woman* (1792), but Emma's remarks are unmistakably close to Wollstonecraft's sentiments: 'When do men *fall-in-love* with sense? When do they, with their superior powers and advantages, turn from the person to the mind? ... Men look for beauty and the simper of good-humoured docility' (*Vindication*, p. 118).

26.   Jane Austen would undoubtedly like to agree with him, and perhaps does in this novel, but still ... there are the Palmers (*Sense and Sensibility*), the Bennets (*Pride and Prejudice*), and even in this novel, John and Isabella Knightley.

27.   In fact, the only character within the novel capable of genuine knight errantry, as opposed to quixotism, is Mr Knightley himself. Harriet absorbs enough of Emma's deepest values to recognise that Mr Knightley's rescue of her on the dance floor from the Eltons' snobbery is the genuine gallant gesture, not Frank Churchill's melodramatic rescue of her from a party of importunate gypsies. Emma has succeeded in teaching Harriet taste, but soon begins to fear that taste will operate against her own (Emma's) interest.

28.   Harriet, like Emma Bovary, attributes romance to objects, which become fetishes. Her 'most precious treasures' include a piece of 'court plaister' from Mr Elton's finger, and Emma thinks to herself, 'I never was equal to this' (p. 265).

29.   He has, for instance, approved earlier her conduct with their nephews and niece, observing, 'If you were as much guided by nature in your estimate of men and women, as little under the power of fancy and whim in your dealings with them, as you are where these children are concerned, we might always think alike' (pp. 75–6). At times, however, her wrongheadedness leads him to understand, in exasperation, why men can be attracted to silly women: 'Upon my word, Emma, to hear you abusing the reason you have, is almost enough to make me think so too [about the masculine preference for Harriet-types]. Better be without sense, than misapply it as you do' (p. 48).

30.   It is comparable in some ways to Emma Bovary's complete self-abandonment when she tries to prostitute herself at the end of the Flaubert novel.

31.   Though on a less grave level, the scene of Emma's final awakening is comparable in effect to Dorothea Brooke's night of agony, spent wrestling with herself after she discovers what she takes to be Will Ladislaw's affair with Rosamond Lydgate, and to Isabel Archer's meditative vigil by the fire after she begins to suspect Osmond and

Madame Merle of having had a clandestine relationship. In all three cases the heroine achieves both a personal catharsis and fellow-feeling for others. Andrew H. Wright, in fact, in *Jane Austen's Novels: A Study in Structure* (London: Chatto and Windus, 1953) sees the 'major theme of Jane Austen's greatest novel' as 'tenderness of heart' (p. 34). Although he claims that Emma possesses this quality in abundance, he says that it is often 'deflected'. As we have seen, Emma herself underestimates her tenderness. The movement of the novel is towards her greater participation in her own schemes.

32.   Nor do the critics agree on how we are to feel towards Emma finally. Mudrick, in *Jane Austen: Irony*, sees the ending as ironic, and Emma as incapable of reform. Some feminist critics, however, resent Emma's submission to Mr Knightley. Alison G. Sulloway, in 'Emma Woodhouse and a Vindication of the Rights of Women', *Wordsworth Circle*, vii, 4 (Autumn 1976), feels the ending is sad because Emma marries 'an utterly traditional man' (p. 332). She is surely missing the point that, within the given social frame, Mr Knightley is the egalitarian and Emma the snob. Nina Auerbach, in 'Austen and Alcott on Matriarchy: New Women or New Wives?', *Novel*, 10 (Fall 1976), would also like to rewrite the ending because she dislikes the implication that, in Austen, women in an almost totally female community 'lead a purgatorial existence together' (p. 12). Lloyd W. Brown gives a more balanced view in 'Jane Austen and the Feminist Tradition', *Nineteenth Century Fiction*, 28 (December 1973) 321–38, recognising that for Austen marriage climaxes an already existing relationship; it does not imprison the heroine in Bluebeard's castle. Juliet McMaster, in 'Love and Pedagogy', Weinsheimer (ed.), *Jane Austen Today*, also stresses that for Austen love is above all an educational process, a beginning, not a feudal ending (p. 89).

33.   Jane Austen, as has often been remarked, details only the unsuccessful proposals (Mr Elton's, Darcy's first proposal to Elizabeth). She suppresses details of successful courtship scenes, not, I think, out of lack of experience or emotional coldness, but the reverse. She seems to suggest that she need say no more to the imaginative reader who empathises with the lovers; for the reader who does not, she would only be wasting her breath. In this case, the lovers' powerful feelings render these two highly articulate individuals awkward and stammering. Emma initially misunderstands and thinks that he is going to ask for Harriet's hand, a realisation of her worst nightmare. She makes the same effort as Dorothea Brooke does to rise beyond selfishness when she thinks Will Ladislaw is Rosamond Lydgate's lover: 'cost her what it would, she would listen'. She listens 'as a friend', and for once Mr Knightley is almost speechless: 'As a friend!... Emma, that I fear is a word. ... Tell me, then, have I no chance of ever succeeding?' (p. 337). Finally, the misunderstanding cleared up, the proposal is as simple, anti-romantic, straightforward and dignified as their earlier exchange at the dance:

'Whom are you going to dance with?' asked Mr Knightley.

> She hesitated a moment, and then replied, 'With you, if you will ask me.'   (p. 256)

34.   These words have been variously interpreted by Booth as a form of the 'apology-by-comparison', which enables Jane Austen to retain the reader's sympathy for Emma (*Rhetoric of Fiction*, p. 263), and by G. Armour Craig in 'The Unpoetic Compromise: on the Relation between Private Vision and Social Order in Nineteenth-Century English Fiction', *Society and Self in the Novel* (New York: English Institute Essays, 1956) as an affirmation comparable to that of George Eliot in *Middlemarch* that too keen perception of the universe surrounding us would be equivalent to hearing the squirrel's heartbeat, and that the price for a total awareness of truth would be a total isolation like that of Jane Eyre (p. 41). It seems to me, however, that in this passage Jane Austen is trying to establish a relationship between her own artistic vision and Emma's, rather than supplying us with a philosophic safety valve about the limitations of human awareness, or warning us against judging Emma too harshly.

Notes to Chapter 3: Emma Bovary

1.   Gustave Flaubert, *Madame Bovary* (Paris: Editions Garnier, 1960) pp. 65–6. All subsequent references to this edition will appear in the text. All translations are mine.
2.   Most translators render 'crotte' as dirt, but Flaubert clearly intended the meaning indicated by the *Dictionnaire Larousse*, the dung of the barnyard.
3.   Martin Turnell, *The Novel in France* (New York: Vintage Books, 1958) p. 269.
4.   Quoted in Martin Turnell, 'Madame Bovary', in *Flaubert: A Collection of Critical Essays*, ed. Raymond Giraud (Englewood Cliffs, N.J.: Prentice-Hall, 1964) p. 111.
5.   Such dreams, comparatively harmless for the wealthy Emma Woodhouse, are dangerous for a girl whose surroundings can never provide even a compromise with fulfilment.
6.   Stendhal, 'Appendice sur *Le Rouge et le Noir*', *Le Rouge et le Noir* (Paris: Editions Garnier, 1960) p. 509.
7.   See Turnell, *The Novel in France*, for an extended discussion of the foot motif.
8.   The flies may also suggest the Furies of classical mythology.
9.   This goes far beyond Emma Woodhouse's wilful self-deception at Box Hill when she steadfastly refuses to believe that Frank Churchill is pretending to look to her for a wife, and not to Harriet Smith.
10.   I am making no attempt to trace in detail the various appearances and functions of these motifs; there have been many studies of this type, notably D. L. Demorest's *L'Expression figurée et symbolique dans l'oeuvre de Gustave Flaubert* (Paris: Louis Conard, 1931). I am merely suggesting the role they play in the fate of the imaginative provincial heroine.

11. She could, in fact, be compared to such Richardsonian heroines as Pamela, with her 'lucky knack of fits', and Clarissa, who dies of a broken heart, or with Austen's Marianne Dashwood in *Sense and Sensibility*.

12. In fact, she never moves beyond Rouen, and that with Léon, not Rodolphe. Rouen is the closest she comes to Venice, for the river made the section of town where Charles received his medical training resemble 'une ignoble petite Venise' (p. 10).

13. Harry Levin, *The Gates of Horn: A Study of Five French Realists* (New York: Oxford University Press, 1963) p. 265.

14. Emma is perhaps here an easy target for those who would read a Lesbian tendency into her behaviour, as Mudrick does with Emma Woodhouse. It seems to me, however, on the basis of the passage from p. 83 quoted in my introduction, that Emma is merely protesting her envy of the power allotted to males by virtue of being male.

15. In much the same manner, one imagines, James's Isabel Archer must sometimes regret having left the house in Albany, where at least she was free to dream. Frédéric Moreau, in Flaubert's own *Education sentimentale*, remembers his happiest experience as having been the decision *not* to enter a bordello when he was still a dreamy youth.

16. Henri Alain-Fournier and Jacques Rivière, *Correspondance*, II (Paris: Gallimard, 1937) pp. 269–70.

17. Flaubert, 'Letters about *Madame Bovary*', in *Madame Bovary*, ed. and trans. by Paul De Man (New York: Norton Critical Edition, 1965) p. 319.

18. Ibid., p. 311.

19. Maybe she has a point at that, in view of recent feminist historians' attempts to re-examine the forgotten half of human history!

20. Flaubert, 'Letters', in De Man (ed.), *Madame Bovary*, p. 316.

21. Ibid., p. 317.

22. The passage is evocative of Flaubert's own sensory creation of the scene in the letter to Louise Colet in which he describes the process by which he becomes not only the lovers, but also the horses, the trees, the shrubbery. One is also strongly reminded of the resemblance between Emma and the boy in James Joyce's short story' 'Araby', in *Dubliners* (New York: Viking Press, 1958), who, shut up alone in an empty room, whispers over and over to himself, as in a prayer or incantation, 'O love! O love!' (p. 31).

23. One is reminded of Jane Austen's Marianne Dashwood in *Sense and Sensibility* (London: Penguin English Library, 1969), who, trying to recover from a broken heart, 'reforms' with characteristically romantic exaggeration. Her sister Elinor smiles 'to see the same eager fancy which had been leading her to the extreme of languid indolence and selfish repining, now at work in introducing excess into a scheme of such rational employment and virtuous self-control' (p. 335).

24. Francis Steegmuller, *Flaubert and Madame Bovary: A Double Portrait* (Boston, Mass.: Houghton Mifflin Sentry Edition, 1970) p. 278.

25.   Ibid.
26.   A student once commented wryly that D. L. Demorest's book (mentioned above) could have been entitled *Statistique Générale de l'expression figurée et symbolique dans l'oeuvre de Gustave Flaubert*.
27.   Quoted in Harry Levin, 'Flaubert: Spleen and Ideal', in Turnell (ed.), *Flaubert: A Collection of Critical Essays*, p. 59.
28.   Matthew Arnold, 'Stanzas from the Grande Chartreuse' (1855) ll. 85–6.
29.   Quoted in 'Contemporary Reactions', in De Man (ed.) *Madame Bovary*, pp. 338–9.
30.   Quoted in 'Introduction', ibid., p. ix.
31.   Matthew Arnold, 'Count Leo Tolstoi', in *Essays in Criticism: Second Series*, ed. S. R. Littlewood (London: Macmillan, 1958) p. 161.
32.   Baudelaire, '*Madame Bovary*, by Gustave Flaubert', in De Man (ed.), *Madame Bovary*, p. 340.
33.   Flaubert, 'Letters', in De Man (ed.), *Madame Bovary*, p. 314.
34.   Anthony Thorlby, *Gustave Flaubert and the Art of Realism* (New Haven, Conn.: Yale University Press, 1957) p. 35.
35.   Flaubert, 'Letters', in De Man (ed.), *Madame Bovary*, p. 309.
36.   Ibid., p. 310.
37.   I doubt personally that he needed this verification since, from all evidence, he had in many ways a 'feminine' (not effeminate) sensibility himself, and could, in fact, be viewed as an androgynous artist.
38.   'Scenarios and Scenes', in De Man (ed.), *Madame Bovary*, p. 279.
39.   B. F. Bart, '*Madame Bovary* after a Century', in '*Madame Bovary' and the Critics*, ed. B. F. Bart (New York: New York University Press, 1966) p. 107.

Notes to Chapter 4: Dorothea Brooke

1.   Gordon S. Haight, 'George Eliot's "eminent failure": Will Ladislaw', in *This Particular Web: Essays on 'Middlemarch'*, ed. Ian Adam (Toronto: University of Toronto Press, 1975) p. 36. Geoffrey Tillotson has said that the only way to overrate *Middlemarch* is to say that 'it was easily the best of the half-dozen best novels of the world' (quoted in Adam, *This Particular Web*, p. ix). D. H. Lawrence has also commented that Eliot does not just (as Henry James claimed) 'set a limit to the old-fashioned English novel'. Rather, she 'started it all. It was she who started putting all the action inside' (quoted by Mark Kinkead-Weekes, 'Introduction', *Twentieth-Century Interpretations of 'The Rainbow'* (Englewood Cliffs, N.J.: Prentice-Hall, 1971) p. 8).
2.   Emily Dickinson, *Complete Poems*, ed. Thomas H. Johnson (Boston, Mass.: Little, Brown, 1960) pp. 263–4. Lee R. Edwards, in 'Women, Energy, and *Middlemarch*', in the Norton Critical Edition of *Middlemarch*, ed. Bert G. Hornback (New York: Norton, 1977), would find many to agree with her statement that Dorothea Brooke is a role model, 'a kind of talisman for many young women' (p. 684).

3. George Eliot, *Middlemarch* (Boston, Mass.: Houghton Mifflin River-side Edition, 1956) p. 468. Hereafter the novel will be cited in the text.

4. David R. Carroll, 'Unity through Analogy: an Interpretation of *Middlemarch*', *Victorian Studies*, II, iv (June 1959) 304–16.

5. Ellen Moers, *Literary Women* (New York: Doubleday, 1976) p. 49.

6. As we have noted, there is a long-standing tradition of creative provincial heroes as well, such as Stendhal's Julien Sorel, but our point is that Dorothea and Emma Bovary are idealistic and quixotic in ways that had hitherto been reserved for male characters. George Eliot is also very conscious that she is rejecting the tradition of 'Silly Novels by Lady Novelists' which she condemned in *The Westminster Review*, 66 (October 1865) 461.

7. Gustave Flaubert, *Madame Bovary* (Paris: Editions Garnier, 1960) p. 68.

8. Quoted by Joan Bennett, *George Eliot: Her Mind and her Art* (Cambridge: Cambridge University Press, 1962) p. 161.

9. Emma Woodhouse is half-orphaned, and Emma Bovary's convent upbringing can be compared to Dorothea's Puritanical education.

10. Paul De Man has also noted, in his Norton Critical Edition of *Madame Bovary* (New York, 1965), that Emma Bovary is similarly restricted by her husband's profession. Charles is only an Officier de Santé, not a medical doctor, and is therefore allowed to practise only in the vicinity of Rouen where the degree was conferred, not in Paris (pp. 7–8).

11. Emma Woodhouse is the only one of the four heroines bumptious enough to dabble in the arts; in painting Harriet Smith's portrait, she is in reality painting her own. Emma Bovary's 'portrait', in keeping with her character, is a miniature that Rodolphe jumbles together with his other souvenirs of cast-off mistresses.

12. Eliot seems to have deleted this passage subsequently because she has a more complex aim than a feminist diatribe.

13. George Eliot, *Daniel Deronda* (New York: Harper Torchbook, 1960) p. 90. This is the phrase Henry James quotes in his Preface to *The Portrait of a Lady*.

14. Quoted by Quentin Anderson, 'George Eliot in *Middlemarch*', in *Discussions of George Eliot* (Boston, Mass.: 1960) p. 90. David Carroll, in '*Middlemarch* and the Externality of Fact', in Adam (ed.), *This Particular Web*, defines 'the reality of the novels' as 'not the mind, not the external – but their meeting place' (p. 78).

15. We are reminded that Dorothea's identity partakes of both the literal meaning of her name, 'gift of God', and the 'dumb Dodo'. In 'Fusing Fact and Myth: the New Reality of *Middlemarch*', Adam (ed.), *This Particular Web*, U. C. Knoepflmacher suggests that Eliot may also have in mind Wordsworth's sister Dorothy as the source of Dorothea's name, adding that in Book x of the 1805 *Prelude* Dorothy Wordsworth is compared to a 'brook' (p. 68). Certainly Eliot underlines the need for the leavening effect of Romanticism in the English provinces.

16.   Henry James, 'George Eliot's *Middlemarch*', in *The Future of the Novel*, ed. Leon Edel (New York: Vintage Books, 1956) p. 81.
17.   Quoted by Joan Bennett in *George Eliot*, p. 162.
18.   Eliot reminds us frequently that Dorothea herself would have been the ideal wife for Lydgate, though Haight at least considers that Dorothea would be unhappy with him and mentions his large, massive hands as the signal of a brutal strength (Adam (ed.), *This Particular Web*, p. 35). I see no sign, however, that the statuesque, healthy Dorothea in any way fears masculine strength, though it may not particularly interest her. Lydgate's brain would be far more likely to attract her. Lydgate's name, incidentally, as Knoepflmacher also notices, was probably suggested by John Lydgate, a contemporary of Chaucer's, who prostituted his poetic talent for patronage.
19.   The inheritance of Stone Court by 'frog-faced' Joshua Rigg deprives Fred Vincy of his 'great expectations'. Bulstrode buys the property from Rigg, and Stone Court subsequently witnesses the drama of Raffles's death, which implicates both the guilty Bulstrode and the innocent Lydgate, and indirectly involves Will Ladislaw whose identity Raffles knows and has used to blackmail Bulstrode. The drama affords Dorothea the opportunity for her one great act of heroism, her defence of Lydgate. Her selflessness in reconciling him with his wife leads ultimately to her own marriage to Will.
20.   We are reminded of the image of Emma Bovary as shopworn picture of a muse.
21.   Mr Limp, the 'meditative shoemaker', has 'weak eyes', and Mr Crabbe, the glazier, 'gathered much news and groped among it dimly' (p. 529). The only good-natured tradesman is, paradoxically, the dyer who, with his crimson hands and their suggestion of devilry, defends Bulstrode and accuses the other Middlemarchers of hypocrisy. (One wonders if he foreshadows Diggory Venn, the reddleman, in Hardy's *Return of the Native*.)
22.   In this respect we might note that the scheming Madame Merle in James's *The Portrait of a Lady* is, like Rosamond Vincy, an accomplished woman who baits her traps well.
23.   Rosamond's hands are always busy with trivial tasks, such as the netting with which, as has been remarked, she symbolically seems to trap Lydgate. In this activity she could be compared to Richardson's Pamela who delays her departure by embroidering a waistcoat for her would-be seducer (I sometimes suspect that, like Penelope, she unravels it every night), or Thackeray's Becky Sharp who is always netting purses.
24.   This 'prostitution' of art in the provinces is in many ways comparable to Emma Bovary's 'piano lessons' which provide an alibi for her rendezvous in Rouen with Léon Dupuis. We are also reminded of Emma Woodhouse's wild imaginings about Jane Fairfax's piano being a gift from Mr Dixon, her best friend's husband.
25.   Not that Celia is like Rosamond; far from dramatising herself, she wears her accomplishments lightly: 'She never could understand how well-bred persons consented to sing and open their mouths in

the ridiculous manner requisite for that vocal exercise' (p. 24). By constantly reminding us of the musicality of Dorothea's voice (like Eliot's own), Eliot suggests that whereas Rosamond and Celia only *play* music, Dorothea *is* music.

26. The architectural imagery may well have inspired James in *The Portrait of a Lady*. Caleb Garth was modelled on George Eliot's own well-loved father, Robert Evans, himself an estate manager.

27. As he admits, 'I live too much with the dead.' Haight notes that Isaac Casaubon, from whom Eliot may have named her Edward Casaubon, was one of the most erudite men of his age, a contemporary of Shakespeare's and sometimes compared to him (p. 52). As Richard Ellmann notes in 'Dorothea's Husbands' (Norton Critical Edition of *Middlemarch*), one of the possible models for Casaubon was Mark Pattison, who authored a life of the Swiss Isaac Casaubon. Lloyd Fernando, in 'Special Pleading and Art in *Middlemarch*: the Relations Between the Sexes' (Norton Critical Edition of *Middlemarch*), speculates that Dorothea's marriage to Casaubon 'in all probability has not been consummated' (p. 695).

28. Osmond's mind, like his house, is perceived by Isabel as 'the house of darkness, the house of dumbness, the house of suffocation'. Emma Bovary sees her future as a corridor with a closed door at the end, and she is constantly exclaiming, 'J'étouffe!'

29. David R. Carroll's article provides an admirable perspective on this notion ('Unity through Analogy'). A less ambitious article by Richard S. Lyons ('The Method of *Middlemarch*', *Nineteenth Century Fiction*, XXI, i (June 1966) 35–47) focusses on the Dagley scene in order to relate it to the themes of the novel, particularly the aesthetic. He concludes that order is to be found in the novel itself, but not in the false art condemned by Dorothea.

30. Dickens's Mrs Jellyby in *Bleak House* provides a corresponding female example of 'telescopic philanthropy'.

31. Her dream of London is not unlike Emma Bovary's of Paris. Bulstrode's wealth is of unsavoury London origin, and Mrs Bulstrode feels that Middlemarch offers 'a better light surely than any thrown in London thoroughfares or dissenting chapel-yards' (p. 449).

32. We are reminded of Emma Woodhouse's imprisonment in a carriage with the egregious Mr Elton making his 'odious' proposal, or of Emma Bovary beginning her liaison with Léon on a mad carriage ride around Rouen.

33. The effect is similar, though the results opposed, to that of Caspar Goodwood's 'lightning-flash' kiss at the end of *The Portrait of a Lady*.

34. George Eliot, *The Mill on the Floss, The Best Known Novels of George Eliot* (New York: Random House Modern Library, n.d.) p. 497.

35. Ralph Waldo Emerson, 'The Poet', *Selections from Ralph Waldo Emerson* (Boston, Mass.: Houghton Mifflin Riverside Edition, 1957) p. 230.

36. Ibid., p. 237. Eliot's attitude towards figurative language is very close to that of the Transcendentalists with whom she was familiar through the Germans as well as Carlyle and Emerson, whom she

once described as 'the first man she had ever seen' (*The George Eliot Letters*, vol. I, ed. Gordon S. Haight (New Haven, Conn.: Yale University Press, 1954–55) p. 20). Her response may have a certain bearing on Dorothea's relationship to James's Isabel Archer, in some ways a Transcendental heroine.

37.   In a sense the one character cut in marble is the intractable Rosamond: she is 'a sculptured Psyche modelled to look another way' from her husband's suffering, in contrast to Dorothea, who is a living, breathing Psyche, or Soul, wedded to a pedantic cadaver.

38.   The scene closely resembles, and may have inspired, Isabel Archer's discovery of Osmond with Madam Merle, he sitting and she standing, which reveals to Isabel that they are, or have been, lovers.

39.   Bennett, *George Eliot*, p. 8. Knoepflmacher (in Adam (ed.), *This Particular Web*, p. 69) also notes the relationship between the art of the novel and 'the roar that lies on the other side of silence'.

40.   Rosamond's attitude towards children is, in fact, much closer to Emma Bovary's.

41.   Most critics have followed Henry James's lead in feeling that Will lacks 'the concentrated fervor essential in the man chosen by so nobly strenuous a heroine' (Edel (ed.), *The Future of the Novel*, p. 85).

42.   It is this empathy which enables her to refuse the uncomprehending Celia's request for the whole story of her engagement to Will: 'No, dear, you would have to *feel* with me, else you would never know' (p. 602).

43.   … or Casaubon's around his of himself as a great scholar, or Brooke's around his of himself as an advanced and powerful thinker. Mary Garth's use of fiction as the vehicle to express this need for tolerance reminds us that George Eliot is using a similar, though more complex vehicle. She suggests that language constitutes the ultimate medium through which empathy can be reached. As Gillian Beer notes, in '*Middlemarch* and "The Lifted Veil"' (Norton Critical Edition), Eliot once wrote in an essay, 'Art is the nearest thing to life; it is a mode of amplifying experience and extending our contact with our fellow-men beyond the bounds of our personal lot' (p. 113). Hornback also quotes her as saying, 'If art does not enlarge men's sympathies, it does nothing morally' (ibid., p. 680). She evidently wanted to link the rational and the emotional (p. 671).

44.   The image can be compared to Stendhal's metaphor for the novel as 'the mirror in the roadway'.

45.   For Emma Bovary, horseback riding, sensual in itself, was just the means to an end – meetings with Rodolphe in the forest.

46.   Joan Bennett, in *George Eliot*, quotes an early letter of the theologically oriented Eliot to demonstrate her extreme asceticism:

   I do not deny that there be many who can partake with a high degree of zest of all the lawful enjoyments the world can offer, and yet live in near communion with their God … but I confess that in my short experience and narrow sphere of action I have never been able to attain to this. I find, as Dr Johnson said respecting his wine, total abstinence much easier than moderation.   (pp. 6–7)

47. The image is similar to that of the cracked cup, James's Madame Merle's ironic symbol for herself (which James was later to reprise in the flawed gilded crystal bowl of *The Golden Bowl*).

48. Barbara Hardy has said, in '*Middlemarch* and the Passions' in (Adam (ed.), *This Particular Web*), that 'Ladislaw's character is the nearest thing in the novel to a portrait of the artist, and a Romantic artist at that' (p. 15). But Will's claim seems no firmer in its foundation than Léon Dupuis's; and it seems clear that Eliot intended Dorothea as her artist figure. Some would argue for Mary Garth, but, as Edwin Kenney, Jr, notes, in 'George Eliot: Through the Looking Glass' (Norton Critical Edition', Mary is too 'limited and static' (p. 739), and Dorothea is 'the character in whom George Eliot participates most imaginatively and intensely' (p. 747). Gillian Beer sees Dorothea as 'an embodiment of poetry' (in Adam (ed.), *This Particular Web*, p. 104), but fails to see that this is not what Dorothea wants, nor probably what her creator would wish for her.

49. Mary Garth's fable is not unlike the tale of Gulliver in the land of the giants.

50. Emma Bovary, too, thinks that if only she could have a son, she could experience masculine adventures vicariously.

51. A twentieth-century Lydgate would probably prescribe Valium for her.

52. This is comparable to James's statement about the open ending of *The Portrait of a Lady*, 'The whole of everything is never told. ... You can only take what groups together.'

53. Henry James, 'Three Reviews: George Eliot's *Middlemarch*', in *The Future of the Novel*, ed. Leon Edel (New York: Vintage Books, 1956) p. 82.

Notes to Chapter 5: Isabel Archer

1. Preface to *The Portrait of a Lady*, ed. Leon Edel (Boston, Mass.: Houghton Mifflin Riverside Edition, 1956) p. 9. Hereafter the Preface will be cited in the text.

2. George Levine, 'Isabel, Gwendolen, and Dorothea', *ELH*, 30, no. 3 (September 1963) 244–57.

3. Henry James, 'Gustave Flaubert', in *The Future of the Novel*, ed. Leon Edel (New York: Vintage Books, 1956) p. 138.

4. Ibid.

5. Henry James, 'Three Reviews: George Eliot's *Middlemarch*', in Edel (ed.), *The Future of the Novel*, p. 81.

6. Ibid., p. 82.

7. Henry James, *The Portrait of a Lady* (Boston, Mass.: Houghton Mifflin Riverside Edition, 1956) p. 54. Hereafter the novel will be cited in the text. This passage is quoted in full in Chapter 1 of this volume, 'Emma's Daughters', p. 1.

8. George Eliot, *Middlemarch* (Boston, Mass.: Houghton Mifflin Riverside Edition, 1956) p. 145.

9.   James, 'Three Reviews', p. 83.
10.   Ibid., p. 82.
11.   Ibid.
12.   Dorothea Brooke has some experience of the Continent as well, in that she was raised partly in Switzerland. But the context is that of a rigorously Puritanical Swiss Calvinism which increased, rather than alleviated her provincialism.
13.   Philip Rahv's chapter, 'The Heiress of All the Ages', in *Image and Idea: Fourteen Essays on Literary Themes*, rev. edn (New York: New Directions, 1957), which also appears in William T. Stafford's *Perspectives on James's 'The Portrait of a Lady': A Collection of Critical Essays* (New York, 1967), focusses on the possibility that 'Isabel Archer is a young lady of an Emersonian cast of mind' (*Perspectives*, p. 141). Richard Chase, in *The American Novel and its Tradition* (New York: Doubleday, 1957), also asserts that her particular brand of romanticism is 'associated with the American tradition of puritanism and transcendentalism' (p. 131). In *The Comic Sense of Henry James* (London: Oxford University Press, 1960), repr. in part in *Twentieth-Century Interpretations of 'The Portrait of a Lady': A Collection of Critical Essays*, ed. Peter Buitenhuis (Englewood Cliffs, N.J.: Prentice-Hall, 1968), Richard Poirier remarks that Isabel's 'action is absolutely within the logic of her Emersonian idealism, so much so that the logic takes its vengeance. In effect she tells the reader, to borrow from "The Transcendentalist", that "you think me the child of my circumstances: I make my circumstance", including, one might add, "my own misery!" ' (p. 35).
14.   R. W. Stallman, in 'The Houses that James Built – *The Portrait of a Lady', Texas Quarterly*, I (Winter 1958) 176–96, also studies the series of houses in the novel, and mentions the relationship between them and James's concept of his work as a fictional edifice. His principal concern, however, seems to be the change in Isabel's character after her marriage to Osmond, which leads her increasingly to 'give herself over' to dark houses and indoor life; he evinces no particular interest in the connections between the architecture in the novel and James's theory of fiction, nor does he mention any possible connection with Emerson's aesthetic theory. Richard Chase also considers the central metaphors in the novel to be those which 'have to do with the house and the garden' (*The American Novel*, p. 127).
         In 'The Flaw in the Portrait', *University of Kansas City Review*, 26 (March 1960) 215–20, Marion Montgomery claims that the architectural metaphor is harmful to the novel since James proceeds from a 'preconceived blueprint'. Montgomery fails to see the analogy to Emersonian organic form, the very reverse of a blueprint. Charles R. Anderson, in 'Person, Place, and Thing in James's *The Portrait of a Lady', Essays on American Literature in Honor of Jay B. Hubbell*, ed. Clarence Gohdes (Durham, N.C.: Duke University Press, 1967), argues that the houses symbolise 'the several stages of Isabel's education' (p. 167), but he takes the same line as Stallman in assuming that the house in Albany, which is 'particularly bleak' (p. 170), is virtually identical to the Roccanera, instead of being its polar

opposite. Moreover, he affirms that Isabel's understanding comes from the imagery alone, indicating that she 'lacks a rational and analytical mind' (p. 166). He fails to perceive that Isabel's mode of 'seeing' moves closer and closer to James's own in the course of the novel. In *The Grasping Imagination: The American Writings of Henry James* (Toronto: University of Toronto Press, 1970), Peter Buitenhuis rightly notes the possible influence of Hawthorne on the house imagery (p. 109).

15.   For a stimulating discussion of 'Madame de Mauves' as an early step in James's path towards the fusion of two cultures in *The Golden Bowl*, see H. A. Bouraoui, 'Henry James and the French Mind: the International Theme in "Madame de Mauves"', *Novel*, IV, 1 (fall 1970) 69–76. Euphemia, convent-educated and, like Emma Bovary or Isabel Archer, raised on books, marries romantically the Baron de Mauves. The Baron, 'a Frenchman to his fingers' ends', loves Euphemia after his fashion – which is to be persistently and systematically unfaithful. Madame de Mauves, like Isabel a Puritanical American, refuses to take the matter lightly. At the end the apparently frivolous Baron commits suicide, and we are left to wonder whether James's disapproval of French sexual standards is not outweighed by his awe at American moral rigidity. In *The American*, Christopher Newman, that Christopher Columbus in reverse on a voyage of discovery to the Old World, abandons his scheme of revenge against the Bellegarde family who have kept Claire de Cintré *née* Bellegarde from him. But Claire herself is walled up forever in a Carmelite convent in the symbolically named rue d'Enfer. The convent bears a remarkable resemblance to the Roccanera, to which Isabel chooses to return at the end of *The Portrait*.

16.   *Middlemarch*, p. 3.

17.   'He endows her ... with the background of his own Albany childhood', according to Edel, in *'The Portrait of a Lady'*, excerpted from *Henry James: The Conquest of London, 1870–81* (Philadelphia and New York: Lippincott, 1962), and repr. in *The Merrill Studies in 'The Portrait of a Lady'*, ed. Lyall Powers (Columbus, Ohio: Charles E. Merrill, 1970) p. 95.

18.   This passage is quoted in full in Chapter 1 in this volume, 'Emma's Daughters', p. 2.

19.   In the name 'Gardencourt', where Isabel is most inclined to see her own nature as 'garden-like', James may have been echoing the name of George Eliot's 'villain' in *Daniel Deronda*, Henleigh Grandcourt, who sees himself as a sort of Machiavellian prince.

20.   Richard Gill, *Happy Rural Seat: The English Country House and the Literary Imagination* (New Haven, Conn.: Yale University Press, 1972) p. 44.

21.   Ibid., p. 45.

22.   Perhaps James was thinking of the eighteenth-century French observer, Moreau de St-Méry, who was shocked to see young American girls sit up late by the fire with their suitor while the

parents went to bed. He was even more shocked that nothing happened, such being the frigidity of American girls!

23. Ralph Waldo Emerson, 'The Poet', *Selections from Ralph Waldo Emerson* (Boston, Mass.: Houghton Mifflin Riverside Edition, 1957): 'For it is not meters, but a meter-making argument that makes a poem, – a thought so passionate and alive that like the spirit of a plant or an animal it has an architecture of its own, and adorns nature with a new thing' (p. 225). In the twentieth century Frank Lloyd Wright gave credit for his own theory of architecture not to other architects but to the great poets of the world, specifically the Transcendentalists Emerson, Thoreau and Whitman.

24. George Eliot also had philosophic and social concerns linked to the English Unitarian radicals, and some of her Transcendental aspirations are reflected in her heroine Dorothea.

25. Dorothea Brooke, in contrast, is concerned with 'widening the skirts of light' for others (p. 813). The unmistakably feminine metaphor applied to both heroines sharpens our sense of how similar they are in conception, and yet how different.

26. In 'James and Emerson: the Lesson of the Master', *The American Scholar*, xxxii, 3 (Summer 1964), Earl Rovit notes that, despite his misgivings about Transcendentalism, James was attracted to Emerson's 'large intellectual space'. On revisiting Concord, James commented, 'not a russet leaf fell for me ... but fell with an Emersonian drop' (p. 440).

27. It is not that Isabel is afraid to explore: if Christopher Newman is a Columbus in reverse, Isabel may well be a Queen Isabella not content merely to stay home and finance someone else's expedition. She seeks 'dangers' and 'sensations', but she flees from any awareness of guilt. Isabel's last name, 'Archer', may suggest the arches of her vaulting aspirations, in particular the arch she is to form connecting Europe and America. Emerson described the Over Soul as 'arching' over men. Its physical counterparts in the novel are the tunnel of the house in Albany, and the dome of St Peter's. The second association of her name is with the Archer, Diana the huntress, goddess of chastity, which may suggest Isabel's wilful innocence, and the virginal quality that has misled more than one critic into thinking her marriage was never consummated. This one aspect of Isabel is closer to Gwendolen Harleth than to Dorothea Brooke: Gwendolen literally participates in an archery meet, dressed in green, and retreats fearfully from sexual passion. Edel, and Quentin Anderson, in 'News of Life' repr. from *The American Henry James* (New Brunswick, N.J.: Rutgers University Press, 1957), also remark on the significance of the Artemis–Diana figure to James, but Anderson proceeds to conclude from this evidence that Isabel has a 'masculine quality' (p. 78).

28. James shared with the Transcendentalists a strong ethical sense, despite his greater awareness of the torment of form. In 'The Art of Fiction' he wrote, 'There is one point at which the moral sense and the artistic sense lie very near together; that is in the light of the very obvious truth that the deepest quality of a work of art will always be

the quality of the mind of the producer' (in Edel (ed.), *The Future of the Novel*, p. 26). He had little interest in the Aesthetic Movement, and once remarked that some French Symbolist poems seemed to him like 'beautifully chiselled vases into which unclean things had been dropped'.

29. We might note that for all of James's admiration of George Eliot herself, it is her massive and 'masculine' weight of intellect he stresses, not her femininity.

30. In 'The Fearful Self', *The Critical Quarterly*, 7 (Autumn 1965) 205–19, repr. in Buitenhuis (ed.), *Twentieth-Century Interpretations*, Tony Tanner considers the architecture in the novel and claims that Isabel's journey is that 'of an uncommitted, undefined self which sets out to find the right house to live in and the right partner to live with'. Tanner also notes that the 'clothes dialogue' is 'a classic formulation of a basic American attitude' (p. 75), but fails to perceive the contradiction between Isabel's expressed attitude and his theory that she is consciously on a quest for the right house and partner from the start. My thesis is that Isabel does not realise that 'the undefined self needs a defining shape' (Tanner, 'The Fearful Self', p. 67), and that she only gradually learns the significance of the 'envelope of circumstances'.

31. Isabel's position seems to echo Thoreau's whimsical assertion that Adam and Eve wore the bower before any other clothes.

32. *Poems of Tennyson*, ed. Jerome H. Buckley (Boston, Mass.: Houghton Mifflin Riverside Edition, 1958) p. 108. Richard Gill also mentions in a footnote on James's 'A Passionate Pilgrim' that 'In the original version Lackley Park was called Lockley Park; Giorgio Melchiori finds in this a possible influence of Tennyson and 'Locksley Hall' (see his 'Locksley Hall Revisited', *Review of English Literature*, VI, 4 (October 1965) pp. 9–25 – p. 269). This further substantiates my theory that James probably had Tennyson's poem in mind in naming Lockleigh (a house that, curiously, Gill never mentions).

33. I wonder also whether, in naming the Misses Molyneux, James may have been recalling Hawthorne's short story about the death of British rule in the American colonies, 'My Kinsman, Major Molineux'. The effect of this reference would be to label the Molyneux sisters (and, by extension, their brother) as anachronisms.

34. It has been suggested that his last name conveys a death image: 'the bones of the world' (see, for instance, Quentin Anderson, in Powers (ed.), *Merrill Studies*, p. 70). If so, James may have had in mind an analogy to that other 'interior decorator', Rosamond Vincy, 'the rose of the world', that 'veritably mulish domestic flower' so brilliantly conceived by George Eliot.

35. Like the French aristocrats, they have made a pact. As the Countess Gemini finally tells Isabel, 'When their little carnival was over they made a bargain that each should give the other complete liberty, but that each should also do everything possible to help the other on' (p. 447).

36. Leon Edel, 'Introduction', *The Portrait of a Lady*, pp. xi–xii, xviii.

37.   Dorothea Krook, 'Two Problems in *The Portrait of a Lady*', in *The Ordeal of Consciousness in Henry James* (New York: Cambridge University Press, 1962) pp. 357–9, repr. in Buitenhuis (ed.), *Twentieth-Century Interpretations*, p. 105.

38.   As Edel remarks, *The Portrait* 'introduced into a Europe that was reading Turgenev and Flaubert, and would soon be reading Tolstoy, a distinctly American heroine' (repr. in Powers (ed.), *Merrill Studies*, p. 104). Comparing her to 'her European sisters', Edel writes, 'Theirs had been largely dramas of love, often of physical passion. Isabel's had been a drama of suppressed passion, passion converted into high ideals and driven by a need for power that reckoned little with the world's harsh realities' (p. 105).

      We never believe Isabel's claim: 'A swift carriage, of a dark night, rattling with four horses over roads that one can't see – that's my idea of happiness' (p. 144). What we do believe is that she has been reading *Madame Bovary*, with its wild, blind carriage ride through the streets of Rouen. Curiously, at least one heroine of passion, Anna Karenina, may, as we have seen, share a common source with Isabel Archer: Eliot's Dorothea. The two-plot novel, the social density and commitment, the religious and philanthropic themes, above all the magnificent heroine, are all reminiscent of *Middlemarch*. But the Russian Anna, unlike the English rose or the American girl, is totally dominated by her passions and only turns to philanthropy (patronage of a hospital) or creativity (like Mary Garth, she writes children's stories) when the affair with Vronsky starts to sour.

39.   The similarity of her situation to James's has tempted some critics (Tanner, Krook) to consider that she has become 'a Jamesian artist' (Tanner, 'Fearful Self', p. 80). There is no evidence, however, that James has changed his mind about denying her the gift of expression. Quentin Anderson is more accurate in recognising that for all the varied roles women play in James's fiction, they never appear 'as creators' (in Powers (ed.), *Merrill Studies*, p. 76). He further speculates that the ending of the novel is unsatisfactory because 'it is impossible to make Isabel Archer over into a man and launch her on the career of an artist' (pp. 77–8). (I will not comment here as to whether the assumption that artistic creativity is masculine is James's or Anderson's.) James's silence on female artists would not seem traceable to any democratic motive, as it seems to be with Austen and Eliot, who are grateful for the combination of circumstances that have privileged them above the lot of even most gifted women. The latter two recognise that for most women the cards are stacked against any concrete creativity other than the biological, and they themselves exemplify the 'trade-off' of domestic conventionality for their craft that Virginia Woolf underlines in *A Room of One's Own* (1929). In the nineteenth century writers like Elizabeth Gaskell, who combined a writing career with mother-hood, were the exception rather than the rule, and she herself wrote poignantly on the difficulties of her situation.

As David Galloway writes, in *Henry James: 'The Portrait of a Lady'* (London: Edward Arnold, 1967), Isabel shares with James's 'artist heroes' the 'desire to "judge" and "choose", to try the resources of her imagination, to break free of limiting conventions – even, indeed, her respect for significant form' (p. 60). Yet his female protagonists lack any power of articulation (with the possible exception of Miriam Rooth in *The Tragic Muse*, but she is an actress, not really a creator). Maggie Verver in *The Golden Bowl* can only be seen as 'the ideal Jamesian artist' (J. A. Ward, *The Search for Form: Studies in the Structure of James's Fiction* (Chapel Hill, N.C.: University of North Carolina Press, 1967) p. 216) at the risk of blurring the distinction between art and life.

40. Gaston Bachelard has pointed out that the Gothic tradition was scarcely the first to discover that locked cupboards, chests, drawers imply secrets and mystery, and Freudian critics add a specifically sexual context to this imagery.

41. If we cannot precisely feel pity for Osmond, it is possible to feel that at times James treats him too harshly, almost as a villain of melodrama, or too allegorically, as in the reference evoking Hawthorne's 'Egotism; or, The Bosom Serpent'. Perhaps the major difference between the endings of *The Portrait* and *The Golden Bowl* is that the Prince, unlike Osmond, is redeemable, and Maggie has something to fight for. Her 'pity and dread' of Amerigo at the end may stem from her awareness that she has let him know how very much she loves him, which puts her in his power in a way that Isabel cannot be with Osmond (or any of the other men in the novel). Osmond's fate is that of a mean mind locked within a generous, philosophic one, and his humiliation cannot be overemphasised. James may be all the harsher on him if Edel is correct in seeing in Osmond 'the hidden side' of James himself: the power drive in the guise of 'meekness and deceptive docility' (in Powers (ed.), *Merrill Studies*, p. 98).

Notes to the Epilogue

1. Henry James, 'Three Reviews', in *The Future of the Novel*, ed. Leon Edel (New York: Vintage Books, 1956) p. 89.
2. Ibid.
3. Quoted by Mark Kinkead-Weekes, 'Introduction', *Twentieth-Century Interpretations of 'The Rainbow'* (Englewood Cliffs, N.J.: Prentice-Hall, 1971) p. 8.
4. Lee R. Edwards, 'Women, Energy, and *Middlemarch*', in *Middlemarch*, ed. Bert G. Hornback (New York: Norton Critical Edition, 1977) p. 684.

Index

164